ripple

A LONG STRANGE SEARCH

FOR A KILLER

JIM COSGROVE

STEER
FORTH
PRESS

STEERFORTH PRESS
LEBANON, NEW HAMPSHIRE

For information about permission to reproduce
selections from this book, write to:
Steerforth Press L.L.C., 31 Hanover Street, Suite 1
Lebanon, New Hampshire 03766

Cataloging-in-Publication Data is available from the Library of Congress

Printed in the United States of America

ISBN 978-1-58642-269-1

1 3 5 7 9 10 8 6 4 2

contents

preface

Twenty-six years. That's how long I've been telling this story. Call it laziness. Or procrastination. Or gut-gripping, mind-paralyzing doubt. Whatever you call it, you'll likely find it at the heart of my sloth-like approach to writing.

I composed a couple of versions — the first for a grad school project, followed by a wonky fictionalized attempt — but my preference has always been to share this tale in person. I've recounted it easily a hundred times while sitting on barstools and at café tables. I shared it with my wife on our first date because she had lived a similar story, and I knew she'd understand. We still half-joke that it's the reason she agreed to go out with me a second time. I told it to a buddy of mine over a bowl of cold borscht in St. Petersburg, Russia. I even stumbled through it in broken Spanish for a young Mexican couple as we rode horseback through a Costa Rican jungle. My nieces used to beg me to share it at family gatherings. I've served it up with whiskey, beer, baba ghanoush, and enchiladas.

I'm a performer. Always have been. As the youngest of eight children, I was birthed right onto a stage with a built-in audience. My ego was nourished with the thrill of connection and the rush of applause. I grew to relish even the slightest reactions of the listeners — the twitchy rise of a brow, a subtle upturn at the corner of the mouth, a slow nod, a muted hum of surprise. I'm still a sucker for their what-ifs and what-abouts that erupt reflexively only to indulge my inner diva and further propel the narrative.

The oral storytelling tradition has allowed for my instinctive omissions and embellishments, according to the temperaments of the crowd. It has left ample latitude for spontaneous changes in tempo, a strategic emphasis on a word, a calculated dramatic pause, or a cryptic hush. The complex choreography among my vocal cords and diaphragm and facial muscles has lent intimacy and authenticity to the story, allowing it to thrive as a living, changing entity.

I feared for too long that committing the story you are about to read to the written page, with all of its perceived permanence, would mute its vibrancy. What I have found instead is the rush of digging deeply into colorful details and the satisfaction of polishing prose. This story is true. I tell it as it unfolded and as it was told to me. While some details are conjecture by those involved, I clearly present them as such.

Much of the dialogue comes directly from my notes and recorded conversations with willing subjects — many of whom are long since dead. Other dialogue was reconstructed from eyewitness accounts and, in some cases, journal entries. And in one instance I have changed names to protect those who requested anonymity.

Like any conscientious journalist, my intention was to keep myself out this story. But as you'll soon discover, I was pulled into the narrative like a rube coerced onto the stage by a magician with a shiny, sharpened saw.

This book had its start at St. Peter's Catholic Church in Kansas City, Missouri, in the fall of 1994. I was in my hometown visiting my mother and had taken her to a weekday morning mass. As we strolled through the courtyard on the way to the parking lot, I paused in front of a statue of a bearded and robed man. His right arm was raised as if he'd just released a dove into the air, and his left hand rested on the head of a dog at his knee.

I read the dedication plate at his feet:

SAN FRANCISCO DE ASIS
In memory of
FRANK McGONIGLE

"Frank McGonigle." I squished up my face as if that would help me think. "I remember when he disappeared. Did they ever find out what happened to him?"

"Oh, yes. It was very sad." My mother slowly shook her head. "They spent nine years looking for him. It was hell for their family. They just dedicated the statue to him last year."

"Hmmm . . ." My brain started popping off ideas as quickly as a flashing string of firecrackers. "Have you ever talked with his parents about it?"

"Sure. They're pretty open about the whole thing. Although it's been awhile since I've seen them. They're such sweet people."

Nearly everyone in Kansas City knows the McGonigle name because they operated one of the finest and most popular meat markets in town for seventy years. Their family was another large Irish Catholic clan in Kansas City's largest Irish Catholic neighborhood. Our parents were friends. They had nine kids; we have eight. Several of them were in school with my siblings, right there at St. Peter's Elementary. Frank was in my brother John's class and about nine years older than me.

"Do you think they would talk to me about Frank?"

"I suppose so. But why?"

"Um . . . just thinkin'."

My mother knew I was always on the hunt for a good story, but what she didn't know was that I had yet to come up with a topic for my master's thesis. While working as a staff writer for the *Albuquerque Journal*, I enrolled in a graduate program at the University of New Mexico. The advisers in the English department allowed me to tailor a program in creative nonfiction writing, as no one had ever requested such a course. Like many things in my life, I made it up as I went along.

The McGonigles agreed to meet with me. Over many months, I interviewed them and their children and others who knew Frank. Over several more months and years, I traveled to the places mentioned in this book and interviewed many other subjects who exhibited varying degrees of reluctance.

When I submitted the final draft of my thesis in the fall of 1995, Joan McGonigle, Frank's mother, asked me to refrain from publishing it as a book. She felt the story delved too deeply into sensitive family subjects that made her uncomfortable. I assured her that I hadn't heard or written about anything that hadn't happened in my own family. And I honored her request.

Sometime in the mid-2000s, a couple of years before Joan died, I saw her at an Easter brunch I attended with my mother and some of her church friends. Joan pulled me aside. "Jim, I've been thinking a lot about the story you wrote about Frank. And I want you to know that you have my blessing to publish it. I'm okay with it."

"Thank you." I hugged her small, sturdy frame. "I know this has dredged up a lot of feelings for you. And I imagine it's probably a little unsettling to think of strangers reading about your family. Frank's story is important."

She just nodded.

PART ONE

ripple in still water

chapter one

If you moved at a steady clip, cut through a few yards, and hopped a couple of fences, you could get from our house to the McGonigles' in about twelve minutes. They lived half a mile from where I grew up in the Brookside neighborhood of Kansas City, and their family looked a lot like ours — big, Irish, and Catholic — as was nearly every other family in our freckle-faced, Friday-fish-eating community.

And if you weren't Irish, well, tough luck. In the blocks surrounding our house lived the Kennedys, McQueenys, McShanes, O'Mearas, O'Sullivans, O'Tooles, Donnellys, Hogans, Hadens, Monaghans, Murphys, and a dozen others, along with a handful of German Irish and French Irish families. On our street alone lived twenty-two kids under the age of seventeen. If a family had fewer than four children, you figured something must have gone wrong. Except for the few "publics," we all went to St. Peter's for church and school. And we walked there and back in gaggles, clogging up the sidewalks.

As a kid, I assumed that if you weren't Catholic, you were Jewish. In our part of town, you were one or the other. I discovered later that most of the white Protestants had fled across the state line into the Kansas suburbs to escape the unrest and tension following the assassination of Dr. Martin Luther King Jr. in 1968 and the failure of voters in 1969 to approve a tax increase for the cash-strapped Kansas City School District. Most of the white Catholics and Jews remained because they had their own schools. I didn't know the few Protestants who stayed, because they didn't have kids. It turns out they were the older couples who yelled at us to get off their lawns.

None of us kids thought it odd that most of the Catholic families were also members of the Jewish Community Center. It's just where we hung out. We were welcomed and comfortable there, and we shared some common bonds with the Jewish kids — an oppressive litany of archaic religious rules, heaps of guilt, and overbearing mothers. Besides, the JCC had a massive outdoor swimming pool and the best baseball league in town with the coolest wool uniforms with stirrup socks.

My parents and the McGonigles' parents were part of the first wave of post–Second Vatican Council "social justice" Catholics. They rallied for peace, protested nuclear weapons proliferation, and worked for racial equality in our city. My father was one of the dozen white lawyers who succeeded in demanding that the local Kansas City Bar Association open membership to African American attorneys. Our parents became active in organizations like Kansas City Crisis, founded in the late 1960s by black and white families dedicated to maintaining positive dialogue. I remember meetings in our house where the kids played upstairs, and the adults met downstairs to address envelopes and engage in spirited discussions. We met in the homes of black families, too — on the "other side" of Troost Avenue, just a mile and a half to the east and the unofficial (yet understood) dividing line between black and white Kansas City. Despite their well-meaning efforts, little progress was made toward integrating our city, and we, the Brookside children, remained blissfully oblivious in our lily-white bubble.

Everyone in our part of Kansas City knew the McGonigles. Aside from their abundant contribution to the human population, the family had a regular place at dinner tables throughout the neighborhood. Sunday's pot roast, Thanksgiving's turkey, and Easter's ham likely came from the meat cases at McGonigle's Market. Their name was synonymous with quality meat. Even their family station wagon was endearingly dubbed the Meat Wagon.

The nine McGonigle children were all older and far cooler than me. They were loud and fun and smart and tough with rapid-fire wits. Many of them were in the same grades as some of my siblings at St. Peter's Elementary School. Mena McGonigle graduated with my sister Mary. Frank was the same age as my brother John. Mark was in Ann's class. Their youngest, Mike, was two years ahead of me, in my sister Sheila's class. I always envied my siblings who had an in with the McGonigle family. Especially my brother Tom. He and Jerry McGonigle were good friends throughout elementary and high school — still are. Jerry passed through our front door and squeezed in at our dinner table dozens of times, and Tom fit right into the McGonigles' pool of testosterone like an honorary brother.

Their home, a two-story stucco house with a broad, L-shaped front porch, stood on a generous, shaded corner lot that was a hub of action in our bustling, kid-infested neighborhood. They were always fielding a game I was too young to play and throwing parties I was too young to attend. And their doors were always open — literally and figuratively.

The McGonigles loved to celebrate, with milestones like baptisms, first communions, and confirmations honored with white dresses, clip-on ties, and huge family receptions. They hosted a notoriously rowdy bingo game every New Year's Eve, and in later years they were known to enthusiastically "hoist a few" in honor of their heritage every seventeenth of March, or on any other day of the year.

Devotion to religion was important. Lots of prayers, rosaries, and masses. And while the kids were still young, all eleven of the McGonigles would cram into a pew at the 8:30 A.M. mass every Sunday at St. Peter's Church about five blocks down Meyer Boulevard from their home.

Frank McGonigle was the sixth of nine children, and, from the beginning, he did things differently. He was the only sibling born backward, and he didn't talk much until he was about three. His sister Joanie said he didn't seem to mind being alone. "He was the only kid I can remember sitting in a playpen and being happy about it."

Joanie and her three sisters helped raise "the boys," as the four youngest were called. Frank came along two years before Jerry, who was one of the most personable kids Joanie could ever remember. Jerry was always smiling, always laughing, always hugging. Frank was sweet in his own way but never pushed himself on anyone.

"I think about the times when those two little kids were sitting there," remembered Joanie with a twinge of regret. "I'd always pick up Jerry because he would smile back at me."

As he got a little older, Frank would entertain himself for hours by dragging an old cardboard box out onto the concrete slab patio in the backyard and sitting in it, looking up at the hazy blue midwestern sky, watching the clouds that slipped by and the treetops that swayed in the wind.

Frank had a few friends in elementary school, but his closest friends, it seems, were his brothers. Competition was constant in their big house on Walnut Street. The four younger McGonigle boys played with a foosball table in the basement — one of those games with the little plastic men on steel rods running through their torsos. They set up leagues and drew up match and playoff schedules. They even named their players and kept statistics on how they performed. Looking back, Jerry, Mark, and Mike all agree that those years seem to be when Frank was happiest.

As the boys grew more coordinated, broom hockey replaced foosball as the sport of choice. The concrete patio in the backyard became the battle rink for these one-on-one showdowns. Players would face off with their brooms, as a designated referee dropped the lid of a mayonnaise jar they used as a puck. Tempers were tested as arms flew and shoulders checked each other. Half-serious fights would erupt to be broken up by the ref.

By the late 1960s, the McGonigle boys, like many kids in Kansas City, were football fanatics, driven by the perennially strong Kansas City Chiefs led by future Hall of Fame quarterback Len Dawson. Frank and his brothers hosted neighborhood football games on the generous strip of grass between the sidewalk and the four-lane boulevard on the south side of the McGonigle house. Frank instituted himself as the all-time punter and kicker and insisted that everyone call him "Jan Frank-erud" after the Chiefs star placekicker Jan Stenerud.

On most summer evenings, the streets and yards of Brookside teemed with impromptu games of Ghost in the Graveyard, Kick the Can, or Flashlight Tag. Inevitably some kid would run home crying because of an unfair ruling or a skinned knee or, like me, with a broken arm after a particularly rowdy round of Red Rover.

What I loved most about those games was that all ages were included. As one of the younger kids, I often teamed up with an older sibling or neighbor who would show me shortcuts and help me over fences. And when the streetlights came on, the excitement intensified — only to be squelched a short time later by the final "Olly, olly oxen free!" that signaled bedtime.

Life was comfortable in Brookside. Each generously apportioned house possessed unique characteristics — modest wood-sided Craftsman bungalows with inviting front porches, half-timbered Tudor Revivals with steep gabled roofs, brick American Georgians with towering chimneys — all solidly built between 1920 and 1935. Soaring oak, elm, and ash trees provided a thick canopy of shade in the summers.

It was the kind of neighborhood where somebody's mom was always home, so if you were playing with kids on another block around lunchtime, you'd eat at their house. And all the moms served the same stuff — peanut butter or bologna or grilled cheese on white bread.

There our lives intertwined, like a big extended family. We learned together, prayed together, and played together. All those people, places, faces, names, experiences, sights, and smells were stewed together, for better or for worse, into a cosmic shepherd's pie.

Our bonds ran deep, and we stayed connected, even after years passed and my family moved a couple of miles away to the outer edge of the neighborhood and my siblings went off to college and moved back home and started careers and got married. The Brookside / St. Peter's ethos was permanently inscribed in our DNA.

So, when Frank McGonigle hopped into his car on a late-spring afternoon in 1982 and drove off without a word to his family, we all felt it. After several days of no communication from Frank, the news began to spread throughout our tight-knit community. Our hearts ached with his family under the weight of their deepest fears. We all began to feel the slow creep of a sympathetic pall settling over our neighborhood, and we all secretly whispered prayers of thanks that this fate had bypassed our doors. Although I didn't know Frank well — he was nine years older — it still felt like one of my own brothers or cousins had gone missing.

After a couple of weeks, we knew something had gone wrong. The faithful legions of church friends and neighbors rallied around the McGonigles by organizing prayer chains and phoning relatives in other cities to look out for Frank. They scoured newspapers from around the country for clues. They began attending Grateful Dead concerts to look for him. They sent out flyers. They shared tears with his mother, Joan, and wrung hands over what-ifs with his father, Bill. They listened and waited and hoped.

Those of us on the periphery did the only thing we were programmed to do in those situations — pray — at our evening meals, before bedtime, and every Sunday at mass. But when months stretched into a year without any clues or reliable leads, those prayers graduated from routine appeals to Jesus, Mary, Joseph, and St. Francis (Frank's namesake) to the serious business of full rosaries and novenas to St. Jude — the patron saint of desperate cases and lost causes.

This went on for nine years.

For nine years the family languished in uncertainty. They searched instinctively and desperately down lonely avenues leading nowhere. They formulated reasonable scenarios of robbery, drug deals, mental breakdowns, and far-fetched theories involving amnesia. Because anything was possible, they held out hope, then gave it up dozens of times and regained it only to lose it again in a continuous, tortuous cycle. They carried on by clinging to those fleeting shreds of optimism and anticipation that Frank would just show up one day and everything would be cool again.

chapter two

For the first time in months, maybe years, Frank McGonigle felt an unfamiliar calm and a flicker of determination as he pulled into a parking spot in front of the bank a few blocks from his house. He smiled because he had a plan — a loose plan, but a plan, nonetheless. He hopped out, strode with purpose to the door, and entered the lobby.

"I'd like to withdraw all my money." He grinned and raised his thick eyebrows at the teller as he slid his passbook and driver's license across the counter.

"Okay. How would you like that? Cashier's check? Cash?"

Thinking sensibly for a moment, Frank asked the teller about converting most of the money into traveler's checks.

"I'm sorry, but the bank officer who handles traveler's checks is off for the day."

"That's fine. I'll just take it in a mix of hundreds, fifties, and twenties."

The teller methodically counted and recounted the $3,800 into three stacks of bills and presented him with a receipt stamped JUNE 7, 1982.

Feeling energized, Frank loped back out to his car with a thick wad of cash, nearly half of which he peeled off and promptly shoved into his left sock. To an otherwise practical person, a stash bulging out of one pant leg might feel a bit uncomfortable and make it difficult to walk, but to Frank, it seemed perfectly logical. He swung back by his house to pack up a few things.

EARLIER THAT MORNING, before dawn, sheets of rain pounded the windows of Frank's second-floor bedroom. Lightning flashed, and thunder rattled the house, but he slept through the ruckus. According to the afternoon edition of *The Kansas City Star*, nearly ninety-mile-an-hour winds swept through the city before 6:00 A.M., leaving about 105,000 homes and businesses without electricity and uprooting hundreds of trees around town.

By the time Frank woke, the McGonigle home on the corner of Meyer Boulevard and Walnut Street was surprisingly quiet. His three younger brothers, who had recently returned home from college, had already left for work at the family market. Frank rolled over and looked at the clock. It was already after ten.

Soft light squeezed in along the edges of the window shades, casting a murky amber haze. Frank dropped his legs over the side of the bed and sat there a second, his long black hair dangling in his face as he massaged his scalp with his fingertips. He swayed as he stood, stretched his lanky body, and breathed in the musk of dried-sweat cotton and the peaty rank of month-old bong water coming from his closet. He pulled on a pair of jeans he had dropped beside the bed and stepped over a heap of clothes his mother had washed and left for him to fold.

He pulled open the door and stepped into the hall. His mother was climbing the stairs with a basket of freshly dried laundry. She hesitated when she saw him, but then continued with what looked like resolution. "Frank, we really need to keep this upstairs clean, since the boys are home," Joan said.

He dismissively backhanded the air between them. "Oh, the boys. The golden boys. Make sure everything's perfect for them."

He made a move to slip past her but stopped. He turned and squinted down at her. "You didn't seem too concerned about me keeping things tidy when it was just me living here. But the superstars are back, so let's polish the joint up."

Joan shook her head. "Frank, you know that's not what I mean."

That look. Those doleful, worried eyes and that tight-lipped disappointment, like she was just about to burst into tears. He wished she wouldn't look that way at him. He'd seen it dozens of times lately, and usually it was served up with a monologue about how she was trying to love him and give him space and maintain a household and some other sort of sentimental rubbish the therapist probably suggested.

"Yeah, yeah, yeah." He waved her off again and shuffled to the bathroom.

Joan left a short time later to run errands for a couple of hours, and when she came back, Frank was gone.

JUST TWO DAYS before Frank left home, he had returned to Kansas City from a hellish three-week road trip to California with his youngest brother, Mike, to visit their siblings Jerry, Mena, and Renee, and to see a Grateful Dead concert in Berkeley. The McGonigle brothers were loyal Deadheads who would catch a show or two every year, mostly around the Midwest. The thought of seeing the Dead in the heart of Deadheadville was to them like planning a trip to Mecca might be for pilgrims. It was one of those road trip stories Mike would retell over and over for years — always with a twinge of pain and guilt.

"The trip was Frank's idea," Mike recalled. "When I got home from college that summer, Frank was trying to talk me into taking my vacation days at the beginning of the summer. I was eager to start working at my dad's store. I had worked my way up to the meat department and was learning the business, so I told him, 'I don't know, Frank. I'm really looking forward to making some money.'"

Frank persisted. "C'mon, man. I'll lend you the money. And you've got the whole rest of the summer to work. It'll be fun. We'll take the back roads all the way to California. We'll see the Badlands, the Rockies, the coast, the Pacific Ocean, the Dead."

Mike had never been west before, so that part intrigued him. But the thought of driving cross-country in a dumpy tin can of a car with a brother who drove him crazy was too much. Sure, they had lots of laughs and some fun times together, but over the previous couple of years, since Frank had dropped out of college and moved back home, he'd become distant and reclusive. Mike often felt uncomfortable around him. Sometimes they had nothing to say to each other.

Mike finally caved and almost immediately dreaded his decision. "I felt sorry for him. Frank really needed that trip as a release from the bullshit he'd been going through at home. He was tired of everybody looking at him and knowing he was troubled. And he needed a break from visiting his therapist a couple times a week."

Frank had recently bought a used four-door Plymouth Horizon with money he saved by working at the family's grocery store. The car had its share of ticks and thumps and squeaks, but it was in pretty good shape. He had it checked out before the trip and bought a brand-new battery for it the day they left.

They departed on Monday, May 17, with the intention of arriving in San Francisco on or before the next Saturday, because their brother Jerry had bought tickets for the Dead's Saturday show. It took them three days to drive across Kansas because of a faulty alternator that continually drained the battery and signaled a warning buzzer that would start with a low, almost imperceptible hum, then crescendo into a loud, head-pounding whine that would go on for hours before they could find a place to fix it. There was a string of costly service stops. Each time they got back on the road with a recharged battery and were feeling good, the buzz would begin. Finally, it was fixed in Idaho Falls, Idaho, but that would not be the end of their troubles, auto-related or otherwise.

"Basically, it was a pie-in-the-sky dream trip that turned into a piece of shit," Mike said. "Each day we thought, *Well, nothing else can happen; let's just have a good time.*"

But there was the speeding ticket in Wyoming and the non-injury (but not non-damaging) fender-bender in Oregon, which meant they had to leave the car to be fixed, rent another car, and drive to San Francisco in time for the show. Then Frank disappeared from the concert and wasn't seen for about four days. He returned to San Francisco in his car with a convoluted story about how he'd met some people from Oregon at the show who gave him a ride back to retrieve the car. They were marijuana farmers who offered him a job, which he considered, but had to decline because he had promised Mike he would return with the car.

When the brothers finally resumed their trek back east along US 40, the car shook so badly from being knocked out of alignment in the accident that it wore out the two front tires. The right front tire blew out just west of Steamboat Springs, Colorado. Although luck had not traveled with them thus far, a bit of it appeared in the form of the Steamboat Tire Company, a service station within coasting distance. They replaced the tires with two lightly treaded used ones, but then the humiliation that finally exhausted Mike's patience occurred. When the mechanic signaled that the car was ready, Frank jumped up into the car, which was still on the rack. Before anyone could stop him, he began to back the car off the rack but somehow managed to drive it diagonally off the side with a deafening crash. The car came to a precarious rest with a metal rod about two inches from piercing the oil pan.

The mechanic screamed. "Goddamn it! What the hell are you doing? I drive the cars off the rack around here."

Mike could see the embarrassment in Frank's eyes, could sense his spirit crushed and defeated. He knew a lot of the crap on the trip was Frank's fault, but he couldn't be too hard on him. Mike wanted to chew out Frank, but he couldn't because he knew his brother was a troubled soul.

Mike wanted to go over to Frank and say, *Hey, it's all right*. And hug him or shake his hand or do something. But at the same time, he was furious with his bumbling brother. "It was like watching a Jerry Lewis movie. I didn't know whether to laugh or cry. I just wanted to crawl under a table because I was so embarrassed for him."

Frank paid the $45.60 bill, and Mike offered to drive. Once they were on the road, Frank curled up in the backseat and fell right to sleep. It was then that Mike decided he could take no more of this hell trip, so he pointed the car in the direction of Kansas City. He knew that if he punched it, he could get back in time to salvage a good weekend, see his girlfriend, and maybe go out Saturday night and drink off the frustrations of the trip with some of his buddies.

Driving east across Kansas on Interstate 70 can be a lonely, monotonous trip. Nothing but flat, windswept fields and farmland from horizon to horizon. Towns pop up in the distance, like metal ducks in a shooting gallery, one grain silo after another. Mike was relieved he'd brought along the boom box he'd received as a high school graduation gift from his parents. It was plugged into the lighter and belting out tunes that kept him company all night. Mike played tape after tape of live bootleg Grateful Dead recordings featuring poorly engineered and rambling versions of "Shakedown Street," "Sugar Magnolia," "Uncle John's Band," and the McGonigle brothers' favorite, "Ripple." He kept the speedometer's needle buried in the red most of the night, well in excess of the car's eighty-five-mile-an-hour top speed, and hit the Kansas City limits just before dawn on Friday, the fourth of June.

"How long have I been sleeping?" came a groggy voice from the backseat.

Frank sat up and looked around as he stretched, his thick black curly hair plastered flat against one side of his head. "Where the hell are we?"

"We're home," said Mike.

"Home? What do you mean, 'home'? What happened to taking the back roads? I thought we were going to see the Badlands?"

Mike was bleary-eyed but resolute. "We're home, Frank. Home. Where we should have been a long time ago. I decided to drive straight through."

Frank punched the back of the driver's seat. "What the fuck, man?"

The two sat in silence as they passed through downtown. When they pulled up in front of the house, Mike summoned a halfhearted apology. "I'm sorry, Frank. I couldn't take it anymore." He climbed the stairs to his bedroom and fell onto his bed in his clothes. He slept late into the afternoon.

When he woke, Mike slowly descended the front stairs hoping to avoid Frank. When he entered the kitchen, he saw his brother sitting at the long rectangular table in the breakfast room. "Hey, Michael. Did you sleep well?"

Mike cocked his head and squinted. "Well, yeah. I guess so. What's up?"

"Not much." Frank smiled, slurping up a spoonful of cereal.

Mike distrusted Frank's friendly mood. Suddenly, it seemed, Frank wasn't upset with him anymore. In fact, all appeared to be fine, almost better than fine, Mike thought. He thought maybe his older brother was working up some retaliation. But looking back, Mike thinks Frank had already made up his mind to leave home.

Frank wiped milk from his chin. "Hey, Dad said it's probably time we stripped and waxed the floors out at the store. It's been a few weeks. I was thinking maybe Sunday would be a good day to do it. What do you think?"

Mike shrugged. "Yeah, sure. I can help you."

The two brothers didn't see each other the rest of the weekend until Mike met Frank out at the store late Sunday morning.

MCGONIGLE'S MARKET ANCHORED the corner of 79th Street and Ward Parkway for nearly seventy years until Mike sold the store in January 2020. The family name still appeared on a sign on the front of the building — MCGONIGLE'S KC BBQ KITCHEN + CATERING — as Mike and his sisters still operated their catering business from an office on the premises.

The grocery and meat market earned its place as a landmark for those who grew up on the south side of Kansas City and a beacon of quality for those who appreciated a superior cut of meat and great service by people who would call you by name after a few visits. The unassuming, one-story brick building had a parking lot big enough for about twenty cars. An illuminated white sign with black letters out front boasted THE FINEST IN MEATS. Above the doors, a banner announced NATIONWIDE STEAK SHIPPING. And on the north side, where the old plate-glass windows had been bricked up, the weekly specials were plastered on hand-painted signs bolted into the mortar.

The McGonigle family provided the main course for holiday feasts, barbecues, elegant dinner celebrations, and late-night left-over sandwiches for three generations. Inside the tightly packed aisles you might find only two brands of peanut butter, but McGonigle's was the best place in town to pick up a thick and tender

Kansas City strip steak, lean sirloins and tenderloins, rotund poul-
try, freshly ground sausages, and succulent slabs of KC-style barbe-
cue slow-cooked in a huge smoker in the parking lot. The market
regularly appeared on "Best of Kansas City" lists as the best butcher
in town.

Bill McGonigle opened the store in 1951. He learned the meat
and grocery business from hanging around his grandfather's meat
company in Kansas City's West Bottoms, near the stockyards. As a
kid, Bill ran a soda stand in his grandfather's store and then came
back to work there as a salesman after flying medal-earning bomb-
ing missions in the Pacific during World War II and marrying his
postwar sweetheart, Joan Wagner. He eventually began selling
produce for a wholesaler and one day called on a small grocery in
South Kansas City that was moving to a new location across the state
line. Bill inquired about taking over the lease on the old building to
start his own business. The rest, he said, is history.

"The best part of owning that store was making it truly a family
business," he said. "Each one of my nine kids grew up working
there — stocking shelves, checking, bagging groceries, and running
deliveries."

Behind Bill's barrel-chested tough exterior thumped the heart of
a saint. And he often extended beatific deeds to his customers, whom
he considered part of his extended family. A regular patron who
lived down the street from the store once ran into severe financial
problems. Bill and some of the checkers noticed that she started
buying cans of cat food even though they were fairly certain she had
no cat. Bill deduced from subtle questioning and intuition that the
cat food was for her. For a few months, until she got back on her feet,
Bill delivered a grocery bag to her home filled with essentials —
eggs, bread, milk, hamburger, and peanut butter. He regularly
allowed customers to carry a tab. The McGonigle family's first tele-
vision was from a customer who lost his job and couldn't pay his bill.
Instead of taking legal action against him, Bill wiped out his debt in
exchange for the TV.

Mike took over daily operation of the store when Bill stepped
aside in 1988 at the age of sixty-nine and with forearms still as big

and solid as the barrel of a baseball bat. Up until his death in 2001, he continued to help during the holidays when the lines to pick up turkeys stretched out into the parking lot.

BY THE TIME Mike arrived at the store on that Sunday afternoon in 1982, Frank had already started working. He had just filled a mop bucket with hot water and was adding some of the liquid floor wax to it.

"Hang on, Frank. What the hell are you doing?" Mike said.

"I'm doin' the floors."

Mike shook his head. "That's not the way you do it, Einstein. You're going to make a mud wax over the top of the floor. It'll be all gray and look like shit."

Frank straightened up and stepped out of the way. "Fine, you smart-ass little shit. Then you do it."

"I will. And I'll do it right." Mike grabbed the mop bucket and dumped its contents down the drain in the janitor's closet, then started refilling it with hot water. Mike held up a bottle of laundry detergent. "This is what you use to clean the floor first. Then you put the wax over the top after it's clean."

"It's a floor, not a pair of jeans. You don't use laundry soap."

"Frank, where the hell you been for the past ten years? We always use this stuff." Mike was starting to lose his patience. He had just spent three weeks putting up with Frank's absentminded, stubborn bullshit and wasn't ready to deal with it again.

"Hey, you think you know more about this store than me? I'm older than you," he said with some satisfaction.

Mike rolled the bucket and mop past Frank and up the aisle to the meat counter, where he began to mop the floor. "You still don't know shit."

"I know the difference between a dirty floor and a pair of jeans. You use wax."

"I know, Frank," Mike said with impatient exasperation. "But you have to clean all the shit off the floor first, so the wax doesn't just mix in and make a sheet of mud."

"You'll see. You just can't admit that my way is quicker."

Mike yelled to the back of the store where Frank was leaning against a produce bin. "Look, there's no point in arguing with you anymore, Frank. So just shut the fuck up."

"No, I won't. I'm going to prove you wrong."

Mike had put up with enough. He dropped the mop on the floor, looked back at his brother, and said, "Frank, why don't you just fuck off and die." He turned around and walked out the front door.

"Those were the last words I ever said to Frank," Mike told me years later. "How was I supposed to know that he was actually going to fuck off and die?"

chapter three

Larry Hyman routinely cruised the sandy roads bisecting Highway 17 Business in Murrells Inlet, South Carolina. Patrolling the bucolic tourist and fishing community — in his own car — was his job as one of two part-time sheriff's deputies. On the morning of June 14, 1982, he received a dispatch with instructions to head over to Nance's Oyster Roast to check out the report of a dead body.

There's no way of knowing exactly what happened next. Hyman is long since deceased. But with information gleaned from the police report and with the help of those who knew the individuals involved and who arrived on the scene within the hour, I was able to piece together a likely scenario.

Nance's restaurant was a well-known family-run business that sat anchored in a wide sunny patch among the trees — a prime location with a stunning view of the pelicans and gulls swooping over the maze of salty creeks that make up the inlet. The building's sun-faded wood siding and the spindles of its inviting front porch bore subtle gouges, chips, and splinters like proud battle scars from their brushes with hurricanes. A brown wooden staircase on the north side of the building led up to the second story and the restaurant's bar. A waist-high pile of discarded oyster shells the length of a fishing skiff had been heaped in the drive out back.

When Deputy Hyman pulled into the parking lot, he was not at all surprised to see Tommy McDowell sitting on the porch steps with his younger cousin Chris Nance. Chris's father, Paul, the restaurant's proprietor, paced the wood planks behind the boys.

Sandy gravel crunched under Hyman's boots as he stepped out of his car. He stood a skinny five-foot-ten in his black pants, white deputy uniform shirt, and black tie. He wore his thinning black hair combed back over protruding ears.

"Hello, Paul."

Paul nodded. "Larry."

The deputy removed his mirrored sunglasses and squinted, directing his attention to the older boy. "So, what is it this time, Tommy?"

The local deputies had seen plenty of Tommy McDowell in the past few years. They had questioned the teenager at least a dozen times for shoplifting, vandalism, stolen checks, a missing dirt bike, and the burning of an abandoned shed. As a minor, Tommy had always weaseled his way out of anything serious, but the stakes had changed since he had recently turned eighteen.

The boy stood and held up his hands in front of him while he rocked back on his heels. "I know what you're thinkin'. I had nothin' to do with it. I swear."

The officer shot a tilted glance at Tommy and shook his head. "Son, I've heard this song and dance before."

"Seriously." Tommy's voice cracked. "Me and Chris were just out in the woods, and I stopped to . . . uh . . . relieve myself and there was a body up against a tree."

Hyman looked at Chris. "That true?"

"Yes, sir," Chris mumbled, looking at his shoes.

"Okay. Fine. Can you show me where it's at?"

Tommy nodded. "Sure. It's just across the road. Won't take but a minute."

"Paul, is it all right if I take these boys with me? You're welcome to join us."

"Fine with me. But I can't leave. Getting ready to open for lunch."

Paul turned to his son Chris. "Go on, now. Show 'em where it's at." Then he pulled Tommy aside by his left shoulder and looked his nephew in the eyes. "You tell Larry exactly what he needs to know."

The two boys rode with the deputy, who radioed his location back to the dispatcher as he turned left down Mariner Avenue. On the northwest corner stood a house that backed up to the woods. It belonged to Bertie Nance, the boys' grandmother. Tommy and Chris had spent much of their childhood in that house and had scrambled through those woods hundreds of times. They knew every path and clearing.

"Stop right up here." Tommy pointed. "You'll have to walk in the rest of the way. The clearin' is up there a ways on the left."

Hyman stepped out of the car and opened the back door for the boys. "C'mon, let's go."

"If it's all right, we'll stay here." Tommy poked a thumb in Chris's direction. "We just . . . can't . . . can't see that again."

"That's fine," Hyman said "But don't go nowhere. We're not finished."

The deputy ducked into the trees and breathed in the familiar dank smell of pine mixed with damp, decaying oak leaves. Following Tommy's direction, he easily located the clearing, where he found the body of a white male propped against the base of a small tree with his legs splayed out in front of him, his head tilted back, and his left arm tucked behind him, almost bracing the weight of his body. The left side of the victim's face teemed with maggots and fire ants. The left shoulder of his white, V-neck cotton T-shirt was crusted purple-black with dried blood.

Hyman was careful not to touch anything as he inspected a ring of white fire bricks surrounding a pile of unburned kindling and a few tree branches. Sticking up out of a hole in one of the bricks was a rolled-up piece of a road map. An unrolled nylon sleeping bag lay in a heap about three feet away near a couple of wadded-up, muddy bedsheets.

When Hyman tramped back out of the woods, the two boys were leaning, arms folded against the patrol car. Not talking, just staring blankly at the ground.

"He's dead, all right," said Hyman. "Looks like he's been here a day or two. Tommy, have you been out here before?"

"Yes, sir. Plenty of times. All the kids 'round here know this place."

"Some of the trees and brush back there look like they've been cut recently. You know anything about that?"

"Yeah. A few weeks ago, Jeff McKenzie borrowed his dad's trac-
tor and cleared out the spot. We been using it as a hangout."

"McKenzie? Is that Leon's boy?"

"Yup. He lives right around here."

Hyman nodded and motioned back over his shoulder toward the
woods. "Do you recognize that guy in there?"

"Never seen him before in my life," Tommy said.

"Okay. I've got to radio this in. And while we wait for the coroner, you two are going to tell me everything you know."

chapter four

For twenty years, Willson "Mack" Williams served as coroner for Georgetown County, South Carolina. There are few days he remembers as vividly as that long-ago June morning.

Mack was sitting in his second-floor office in the county courthouse on Screven Street in the historic district of Georgetown when he heard a knock at the door. He took a drag off his cigarette. "Come on in."

Doris Simmons, the secretary for the Georgetown County sheriff, opened the door wide enough to peek her head through. "Morning, Mack."

"Hello, Doris. What can I do for you?"

"Well, since the phones got knocked out by the storm yesterday, the sheriff asked me to come over here and get you. He wants to see you in his office right away."

"Okay. Do you know what's going on?"

"He didn't say, but he seemed pretty urgent about it."

"A'right, then. I'll walk back over with you." He snuffed out his cigarette in an ashtray and gathered up some papers.

Mack was not a tall man — slender with thin, graying hair, glasses, and a few rose-colored spots on his forehead and nose from where skin cancers had been removed. In his capacity as coroner, he always wore a shirt and tie. He preferred short sleeves, no matter the season.

The office of county coroner was established by the framers of the South Carolina state constitution. As a public officer, the coroner is technically over the sheriff and the only one who can arrest a sheriff. Mack worked closely with three different sheriffs during his tenure and never had to serve papers to any of them.

Mack walked across the street to the sheriff's office, where he learned that someone had called from Nance's Oyster Roast in Murrells Inlet to report a dead body. Later, a deputy who had been dispatched to the scene radioed Sheriff Michael Carter to verify that there was indeed a body of an unidentified white male. Sheriff Carter dispatched Agent John Leath of the South Carolina Law Enforcement Division (SLED) to transport Mack to the scene and assist in the investigation.

Driving north out of Georgetown toward Murrell's Inlet on Highway 17, Agent Leath and Mack crossed two bridges spanning gold-and-green-reeded marshland at the confluence of the Black and Waccamaw Rivers. Shrimp boats with nets hanging from their masts like tattered scarecrows bobbed about their moors in the mouth of the rivers. The road was lined with densely wooded pine forest on either side all the way up past Pawleys Island and through Litchfield Beach. Thick underbrush of creeping ivy and kudzu covered the sandy soil. Where Highway 17 Business veered off from the main road on the south side of Murrells Inlet, a billboard welcomed them to town: MURRELLS INLET SEAFOOD CAPITAL OF SOUTH CAROLINA.

Nance's was about a mile and a half down Business 17 on the right. Mack and Agent Leath pulled into the parking lot, where they met Deputy Hyman. He escorted them across the road to the woods.

After arriving in the clearing through the damp brush and sandy mud, Mack pulled out his notepad and began to write. "At the scene we found the body of a white male. Due to condition of the body, it was impossible to tell immediately the cause of death."

Walking around on a thick bed of leaf mulch, Mack found it difficult to determine much of anything — whether the body had been dragged, and if there was a weapon or any shell casings. He always carried a Polaroid camera with him to take pictures of crime scenes, so he rattled off about five pictures of the body and the surrounding area. The camera's flash hadn't been working very well, so the pictures turned out dark, with bright spots where the sun shone through the thick canopy of leaves. "John, what do you think about getting a lab team down here to look over the scene before we remove this body?"

"Well, since that storm blew through here over the weekend, there doesn't seem to be a whole lot for them to work with." Leath kicked at some vines. "And this underbrush is so damn thick, they couldn't find much anyway. I say we just get the body out of here."

It had rained so hard over the weekend that it halted play at the Lipton Iced Tea Mixed Doubles Championship at the nearby Litchfield Country Club. A local newspaper described the weather as marked by high winds and heavy afternoon "tornado-like thunderstorms."

The two men drove back across the road to Nance's restaurant, where Mack phoned Sheriff Carter and advised him of the situation and their decision to bypass an investigation by the lab team. They decided that, if needed, deputies could return later with metal detectors to sweep the area for shell casings or bullets. Mack requested an ambulance, which arrived in Murrells Inlet about two o'clock. After EMTs loaded the body, Mack instructed the driver to go to the Georgetown County Memorial Hospital and wait for him there.

Before leaving for Georgetown, Mack gathered all the items left at the scene and itemized them in his notebook — a sleeping bag stuffed into a blue nylon duffel bag, two bedsheets, a beer can, and a section of a road map of the San Francisco Bay Area that appeared to be torn from an atlas. No wallet, no identification, no keys, no backpack, no suitcase.

"I've got a funny feeling about this one, John," Mack said to Leath as they walked to the state-issued sedan. Mack dropped into the passenger seat, lit a cigarette with his silver Zippo, and settled in for the thirty-minute drive back to Georgetown. "Nobody around here seems to know who this boy is. That's a first for me. Since I've been coroner, we've never had a John Doe."

Leath nodded and let out a slow whistle. "Just be glad you don't have an interstate running through here, or you'd see plenty of 'em."

Mack gazed out the window at the blur of lush green vegetation. He exhaled smoke and absently tapped his temple with his forefinger, then whispered to no one in particular, "This young man must be somebody's son. Somebody's brother. There must be somebody look-ing for him. I'm gonna find his family."

Mack knew about family. He had a wife and young son, and, as coroner, he worked regularly with distraught families. When he took over the job in 1977, he thought he had all the answers to the coroner business. After being on call twenty-four hours a day, 365 days a year, he realized he didn't know squat.

He arrived in Georgetown in 1959 as a twenty-one-year-old with-out a college degree. He dropped out of The Citadel in Charleston after the first semester of his junior year and struck out on his own, moving to Georgetown, where he assured his parents that he would get a job at a funeral home. He had no experience in the business; he just thought he might like it. Mack showed up at the door of the Mayer Funeral Home and convinced Mr. Mayer to give him an apprenticeship. Mack did his two years as an apprentice, and in 1961 he went to embalmer's school in Dallas. In March 1962, he came back to work for Mayer Funeral Home, and, when Mr. Mayer died shortly after that, he moved into the apartment over the funeral home where he and his wife, Ann, raised their son, Willson Jr., and where they lived through his tenure as coroner.

When I met Mack in 1995, he exuded compassion and sincerity. You could see it in the gleam of his pale-blue eyes; in the way he looked at people with a half-cocked smile; in the way he talked to his son so lovingly on the phone and called Ann "my lovely bride," and meant it. He spoke harshly about no one, and when it came to people whom most everybody else in town was bad-mouthing, Mack refrained from gossip.

His voice dripped with the melody of his South Carolina upbring-ing as it meandered like a country-western song through run-on sentences. He tapped his unlit cigarettes on the table before slipping them into his mouth with his thumb and forefinger and would tell you with an infectious, gravelly smoker's chuckle and a glimmer in his eye that he was "the best-lookin' fifty-seven-year-old you ever did see."

He would also tell you that he could write a book about all the wild cases he's been involved in as county coroner, but there had been none quite so unusual and troublesome as the case of the "boy in the woods."

WHEN MACK ARRIVED at the hospital about an hour later, he met with the pathologist, who recommended that, due to its condition and the circumstances surrounding its discovery, the body be transported to the medical examiner's office at the Medical University of South Carolina in Charleston, about sixty miles south of Georgetown. It was there that Dr. Sandra Conradi performed the autopsy the next day. The following are her notes:

> The unembalmed body is that of a thin, well-developed adult white male in his twenties, measuring approximately 69 inches and weighing approximately 161 pounds. His hair is moderately long, dark brown and in a male distribution. He's clothed in a light blue, knit shirt, faded blue denim trousers, a brown belt — a broad brown belt with a weave pattern on it and a large, yellow metal buckle. White brief under shorts, white socks with the right side having yellow and blue stripes, and the left red and blue stripes, and blue Kangaroos running shoes. Twenty-four cents and a blue golf tee are in his pocket.

Years later, Frank's mother told me, "It was just like Frank to wear mismatched socks."

The autopsy went on to verify two gunshot wounds.

> The first one entered through the left eye and was directed backward twenty degrees upward and twenty degrees to the right through the middle portion of the brain. A .25 caliber copperjacketed bullet was found in the calvarium. A second, graze-type wound was found adjacent to it on the left cheek with only superficial injury. Soot powder and charring were not positively identified with either wound (which rules out self-infliction). These findings would indicate that death occurred two–three days before autopsy.

Avidity indicated that he was in a sitting position for at least four hours after death.

Just before ten o'clock on Tuesday morning, June 15, Dr. Conradi called Mack from the autopsy room to relay her findings. She added to her report that no cuts, abrasions, or bruises were found on the body, other than the two gunshot wounds. Also, she said the victim's teeth were being removed for study and evaluation and fingerprints had been lifted. These items, she said, along with the bullet and clothing, would be stored in the medical examiner's office if Mack needed them.

Later that afternoon, an agent from the SLED office in Columbia called Mack, requesting that the medical university send him mounted and developed color slide film of Frank's body and that the SLED office would make a black-and-white photo from them to be used in the flyer being sent out nationwide on their computer network. The agent also requested that the fingerprints be sent along with the photographs, feeling that this would be the best shot at identification.

That same day, the *Georgetown Times*, the county's twice-weekly newspaper, ran a small article, with the headline "Body of Man Found at Inlet in Woods," on page ten, next to a photograph of the new Miss Georgetown County, who had been crowned at the Howard High School auditorium a few days earlier.

The article quoted Sheriff Michael Carter. "As it stands now, whether any foul play is involved cannot be determined."

Two days later, that changed.

The Georgetown Times
THURSDAY, JUNE 17, 1982
Officials: Man's Death Homicide
Authorities say the death of an unidentified white man whose body was found in a wooded area at Murrells Inlet Monday morning is a homicide case.

Georgetown County Coroner Willson M. Williams said the man, who appears to be in his early twenties, was shot twice in the head. Officials believe that the body has been in the area for approximately two to three days.

An autopsy on the body will be performed by pathologists at the Medical University of South Carolina to determine the cause of death.

The local sheriff's department and an agent from the South Carolina Law Enforcement Division (SLED) are still searching for the man's identity and clues surrounding his death. The body was discovered by two men walking through a wooded area between U.S. Highway 17 business district and U.S. Highway 17 by-pass.

Officials described the victim as five feet, nine inches tall, weighing 160 pounds, a small mustache and medium long black hair.

Carter said the body was clad in a short sleeve tee shirt with white on the upper half and blue on the lower half. The sleeves and the collar of the shirt were also trimmed in blue.

The victim was wearing blue jeans with a brown leather big buckle belt, white socks and tennis shoes. He was also carrying a blue duffel bag.

Officials are asking anyone with information pertaining to the subject to contact the sheriff's department.

chapter five

"Bull-she-it. Total bull-she-it." Chris Nance shook his head and ran his hand through his neatly trimmed brown hair. "That ain't how it happened at all."

I met Chris outside his family's restaurant on my first visit to Murrells Inlet, in February 1995. Earlier that week I had embarked on a mission to retrace Frank's likely twelve-hundred-mile route from Kansas City to the Carolina coast with the intention of digging up some answers surrounding one of the most indelible mysteries of our Brookside Irish Catholic community. At the very least, I wanted to help Frank's family gain some closure. I had no idea his story would become such a prominent chapter in mine.

Chris and I stood in the glare of the restaurant's parking lot covered with thousands of broken, sun-bleached oyster shells that crunched under my hiking boots. He was a polite, smooth-talking twenty-seven-year-old with pale-green eyes and a high-pitched southern voice that turned up at the end of sentences, like he was asking questions all the time. He seemed relaxed enough, but he kept running his left hand through his hair. And he immediately adopted a folksy habit of calling me "Bubba" that was mildly endearing the first few times.

"The police report says you two were out in the woods together when you found the body. And Tommy's mother told me the same thing."

Chris winced and shook his head. "A'right now, Bubba, I know what it says. But let's cut through the chitlins. Tommy was a first-class bull-shitta'. They ate up ever'thang he told 'em."

"So, he lied about the whole thing?"

"Most of it. Hell, he lied about ever'thang. First off, I wadn't even with Tommy. Didn't know anythang 'bout it, until after he found the body."

"So, when did you first hear about it?"

Chris turned and pointed. "I was sittin' on a bench right out here in front of the restaurant with Ernest Myers. He was the colored fella who worked for me."

"Wait, weren't you like fourteen at the time?"

"Yup, that's 'bout right."

"And you had somebody working for you?"

Chris repositioned his stance and glanced at the ground. "Well, he actually worked for my daddy. And . . . well . . . uh . . . my daddy kinda gave him to me."

I raised my eyebrows. "Gave him to you?"

"Well, to help me with my chores and whatever other work there was . . . ya know."

Actually, I didn't know. Those types of arrangements of chattel servitude didn't exist in my insulated midwestern world. I also didn't know how to respond. I just shuddered and nodded in awkward disbelief. "Uh-huh."

"So, Tommy pulled up in front of the restaurant in his li'l red pickup and said, 'Hey, I found a body in the woods. You guys want to come see it?' A' course, we thought he was bullshittin' us, but he swore up and down and told me to get in the cab with him."

"Did Ernest go with you?"

"Yessir. A' course, he rode in the back."

Somehow the unapologetic racism was becoming less surprising. "Of course."

"When we got over there, Tommy and Ernest went into the woods ahead of me and into the clearin' where the body was. I held back, but I could see the body through the trees. That's all I wanted to see. I didn't want to get any closer."

"So, then what?"

He shrugged. "We came back here to call the sheriff."

"Why did Tommy show you the body first, before calling the police?"

"Hell if I know. Tommy was creepy and obsessed with death."

"Is Ernest still around? You think he'd talk to me?"

"Naw, he died a few years ago."

"How convenient."

Chris nodded and shrugged. "Yup."

I couldn't stand any longer in the glaring sun of the parking lot, so I suggested we sit down in the shade of the restaurant's front porch.

"So, do you think Tommy killed the boy in the woods?"

"Don' know fo sho', but I have my theories."

"Like?"

Chris shifted his gaze from me, past my shoulder, to the woods across the road. "The only thang I can come up with is that Tommy tried to rob 'im, or tried to fuck 'im, and it went bad."

"You really think Tommy was capable of committing murder?"

"That boy was cold. No heart at all. He had nothin' but a thumpin' gizzard."

A few years before I met Chris, the sheriff's department stepped up their investigation when the "boy in the woods" was identified as Frank McGonigle. The detectives questioned everyone involved for a second time. Chris fully cooperated. "I wanted to set things straight. And shortly after I gave 'em my statement, I got a call from my daddy. He said, 'Chris, what the hell you been tellin' people?' I said, 'I'm tellin' the truth.' And then he said, 'Remember, you're a suspect in this thing, too. You could get the rap for this if you don't watch it. You could go to prison.' I took that as a threat."

Paul Nance excelled at leveling threats. Every person I spoke to in Murrells Inlet said the same things. Paul was an asshole. He was ruthless. He was abusive. He was feared.

One local man reached out to me with his stories about Paul but preferred to remain anonymous. He grew up in Murrells Inlet and worked at a local business owned by his father. He remembers Paul driving around town in his eighteen-foot black Cadillac Fleetwood Brougham with its lipstick-red interior. "No matter where he went — the fish market, the convenience store, the gas station — he'd pull up and blow the horn until someone ran out to take his order or pump his gas. Hell, he never got outta that car. That's just the kind of guy he was, lazy and expected everyone to wait on him."

Not one person I interviewed denied that Paul Nance had a finger in everything that happened in town. He ran drugs in on his fishing boats and distributed them up and down the coast along with oysters and clams. He dabbled in gambling operations. He also owned the majority of the shell-fishing rights around Murrells Inlet, so he would lease those rights to others, and he would buy oysters and shrimp from them — further clamping his grip on the lives of so many families in town and putting a small navy of captains under his thumb. To expedite business deals, he employed the services of a couple of local thugs who would rough people up, break some bones, or worse, all at Paul's behest.

"Yup, all that's true." Chris Nance slowly shook his head with a twinge of disgust. "I guess you could say my daddy was . . . uh . . . notorious."

Somehow Paul skated and skirted the law and was never charged with a crime. A few of his employees were intercepted transporting drugs in on one of his shrimp boats. They all went to jail denying Paul's involvement, testifying that they "borrowed" the boat without Paul's knowledge. Everyone in town knew the truth. Even the cops.

Joey Howell was another part-time deputy who patrolled and lived in Murrells Inlet. He, too, had many run-ins with Paul. "We all knew what he was up to, but we were never able to pin anything on him. And it wasn't for lack of trying. He kept his hands clean and got other people to do his dirty work. He was just that slick."

With only seventeen deputies — many of them part-time — to patrol a thousand square miles, the Georgetown County Sheriff's Department had a hard time keeping up. It was so small and under-funded that deputies were issued only guns, white uniform shirts, and hats. They had to provide their own black pants and drive their own cars. Howell dipped into his own pocket to install a blue, rotating beacon light on top of his powder-blue 1979 Ford Fairlane. Aside from his professional competence and his loyalty to the badge, he carried himself with the patient gentleness of a preacher and never once showed exasperation from my years of persistent questioning.

"Do you think Paul had anything do with this case?" I asked.

"One of many rumors that sprang up around town is that Paul Nance had the boy in the woods killed over some drug-related disagreement," Howell said as he raised his bushy eyebrows. "But we'll never know."

I did find one person who had something nice to say about Paul. He only agreed to speak to me if I didn't use his name. I also met him in the parking lot of Nance's restaurant. He spoke quickly and quietly while his eyes flitted around our periphery as if Paul, who had been dead for four months, might hear us. "I used to work for Paul Nance. My daddy worked for Paul Nance. So did my uncles and my cousins. Hell, ever'body in this town work for Paul Nance. I had a few boss-men in my time, but none like him." Then he pointed to the restaurant. "His heart was as big as that building."

Chris Nance didn't deny the deep, tight-lipped loyalty surrounding his father. He just wanted to make it perfectly clear that Paul premeditatively and pathologically designed that loyalty by paying his associates well, in cash, and intimidating the hell out of them.

"The word around town was, 'Don't fuck with Paul Nance.' So, as a kid I could hardly find anybody to play with me. It was like the Murrells Inlet Mafia or something. He was very powerful." Chris paused and released a wispy sigh through his nose. "There are some decent people in this fam'ly who don't want to be put in the same class as my daddy. I consider myself one of 'em."

Chris claimed his and Tommy's grandmother, Bertie Leona Nance, knew something about the murder, too, but whatever she knew went with her to the grave in the early 1980s. She lived in the red-brick house on the corner of Mariner and Business 17, across the street from the restaurant and at the edge of the woods, about a hundred yards from where they found Frank.

"My grandma was very close to my cousin Tommy, maybe too close," Chris said. "Tommy stayed over there with her when things weren't going well at home. He took advantage of her kindness, but he could do no wrong in her eyes. Hell, he went as far as to write checks on her bank account while she was on her deathbed."

According to the sheriff's investigation, Grandma Nance had owned a .25-caliber pistol but gave it to Tommy in exchange for a shotgun a couple of weeks before Frank had been shot with a .25-caliber pistol. A couple of witnesses denied she owned a handgun but acknowledged that Paul Nance had given his mother a shotgun for protection since she and her sister lived alone in the house. Others confirmed the existence of a pistol and implied that Grandma Nance had withheld information about the gun and that she may have disposed of it sometime after it became potential evidence.

When I told Chris about the report's findings, he raised his brows and smiled. "I thought the family were the only ones who knew about that gun."

"What do you know about it?"

Chris jerked his head back behind us toward the ocean. "All I know is that gun's probably out in the Gulf Stream somewhere." Then he shot me a sideways glance and slightly shook his head. "There's a lot of people around here with blood on their hands."

chapter six

The town of Murrells Inlet lies between the Waccamaw River and the Atlantic Ocean, about thirteen miles south of Myrtle Beach's assaulting neon bustle. You won't find high-rise hotels or mega-mini-golf complexes or an oppressive number of T-shirt shops in Murrells Inlet. In 1995, it was quaint and quiet with an oyster-slurping, beer-drinking, back-porch kind of vibe. A smattering of well-established seafood restaurants and markets dotted the main road amid well-appointed waterfront estates featuring pleasant views of the surrounding natural saltwater estuary. Since then, the population has nearly doubled to ninety-one hundred, and hundreds of new condominiums have sprung up. In the late 1990s, the excitement cranked up a few notches with the opening of the Murrells Inlet MarshWalk, a half-mile boardwalk humming with themed bars and restaurants.

The Inlet, as the locals call their unincorporated community, holds distinction as the northern gateway to what has more recently been dubbed the Hammock Coast. As the state's oldest fishing village, it dates back to the early 1730s when Captain John Murrell (also spelled Morrell and Murrel on some maps) bought 2,340 acres and built a house on a bluff overlooking what would become the massive Wachesaw and Richmond Hill rice plantations and, a couple hundred years later, a sprawling golf club. From the late 1600s to the mid-1800s, more than one hundred rice plantations dominated and fueled wealth in South Carolina's Lowcountry. Other successful industries like indigo, logging, cotton, and caviar thrived in the area, but nothing came close to rice as the dominant cash crop, which helped make Charleston one of the richest cities in the colonies during those years. Several factors precipitated the collapse of South Carolina's rice industry, including a string of intense Atlantic hurricane seasons and increased competition from Gulf states, but none bigger than the abolition of slavery.

Long before the arrival of Captain Murrell and other Europeans, native people, including the Pee Dees, Seewees, Sampits, Santees, Winyahs, and Waccamaws, inhabited the land. They built longhouses from pine and palmetto and lived off the bounty from the saltwater creeks and freshwater rivers while toughing out the mosquitoes and hurricanes. The Waccamaws referred to their native land as Wachesaw, which a few dubious online sources claim to translate as "place of great weeping," perhaps because of the indigenous burial sites discovered in the area. A fitting name for a place that has seen its share of oppression and violence.

When President Benjamin Harrison established the Board on Geographic Names in 1890, it proposed eliminating apostrophes from town names. Removing the possessive, the board contended, would be easier for mapmakers and the postal service, and it would eliminate the implication of private ownership of a public place. So, Murrell's became Murrells — forever rankling the punctuation sensibilities of grammar geeks like me.

According to more recent and trivial folklore, locals claim Murrells Inlet as the birthplace of hushpuppies. Not the shoes, but the deep-fried balls of cornmeal served as a side dish to fried fish, fried clams, and fried shrimp. I suppose every town needs a claim to fame. Even today, beneath its veneer of southern charm, Murrells Inlet emits an alluring siren's song that attracts strangers and just plain strangeness. For centuries, this town has beckoned a steady stream of meandering souls — ebbing and flowing like the tidal foam that tiptoes into the secluded coves and creeks every day and slinks unnoticed back out to sea. Some linger to soak in the sunshine and wide alabaster beaches of the Grand Strand, play some golf, and make it just one more day. Others take opportunistic pit stops before skittering off into the darkness. It seems even the indigenous people sensed the movement and transience of this place, as their name, and that of the river, Waccamaw, purportedly translates as "coming and going."

About three miles east of the river is the inlet itself. As the name implies, it's a narrow coastal recess providing inland access along the Atlantic shoreline. From the air, its winding labyrinth of creeks looks like the sprawling tentacles of a sea creature or an artist's rendering of your small intestine. Multiple meandering arms of the Main Creek, Oaks Creek, and Woodland Creek create a perfect environment for sailors seeking a break from buffeting winds or bandits looking for a place to hide.

"This is a pirate town. Always has been, and still is — in its own way," said a guy named Jimmy with a noticeable puff of his chest. He was into his third bottle of Bud Light at the Thirsty Whale, a gritty tavern that has since been razed and replaced with condos. "But most people around here are honest taxpayers and good Republicans."

I like gritty bars. It's where I meet the most interesting characters and get the best information — the juicy bits that others might prefer to sanitize. And sometimes those bits turn out to be true.

Four other guys sat at the worn wooden bar that afternoon. All but Jimmy wore dirty ball caps with faded logos, and they all shared the deep-red, sun-leathered skin of fishermen. Shell fishermen.

Jimmy's face lit up like a child recounting the plot of his favorite cartoon. "This is an inlet, right? So, we got some natural p'tection from the sea. That's why pirates loved this place. You ever hear of Drunken Jack?"

"No, but I'd like to."

"Yeah, well he used to run with Cap'n Kidd. I know you heard a' him. My daddy'd tell me stories about how they sailed in here and buried their loot. You won't find that in history books, but what do they know?" He waved his beer bottle at no one in particular.

Hard-nosed historians scoff at the baseless pirate tales, but the locals don't care. It makes for good barstool talk.

Jimmy inspired me to read up on local pirate lore, and I found a character who sounded familiar. Blackbeard. A.k.a. Edward Teach. He led a reign of piracy along the Carolina coast, including the blockade of the port of Charles Town (now Charleston) to the south in 1718. Many believe he liked to hide out in the maze of creeks around Murrells Inlet, but that's mostly wishful thinking.

However, historians do agree that throughout the Civil War, the inlet provided perfect cover for blockade-runners to surreptitiously dock and off-load food and weapons delivered to the rebels. After the dawn of the twentieth century, Prohibition provided a bountiful backdrop for freebooters, and Murrells Inlet quickly earned a reputation as an ideal place for rumrunners to illegally distribute corn liquor throughout the South. Drugs eventually took over as the popular contraband. Marijuana, cocaine, or whatever high you wanted all came ashore here on local shrimp boats and small muscle-powered rowboats.

By the 1970s and '80s, Murrells Inlet became a popular spot for drug dealers and troublemakers. And with the county line running through the north side of town, legal jurisdiction was conveniently sketchy. It was the kind of place where you could get away with just about anything.

"Lot of weird shit happenin' in this town back then," said a guy known as Rooster, who was a cook at a local seafood shack. I met him while he was taking a smoke break out back. "We've had drug rings, small-town organized crime, crooked cops, family fights, like when the Scott brothers started shootin' at each other up at their house. Billy ended up dead, and Eddie went to prison."

"Sound like nice guys," I said.

"Aw, that ain't the half of it. We also had the incident with Joseph Pickett. He got cut up with a chain saw."

"Damn, that's cold-blooded."

Rooster chuckled. "We got a sayin' 'round here: 'Three goin' down to the creek by lantern, and two comin' back in the dark.'"

My eyes widened and brows lifted. I never had much of a poker face. It certainly looked like Rooster was taking delight in my discomfort.

"Hell, we had people fed to the gators that ain't never been found." Then, with a studied expression of understatement, he added, "Life in these parts can be a gamble."

It can also be a sure bet for those who love natural beauty — a paradise for bird-watchers and anglers and artists and lovers — with the kinds of sights and sounds and smells that make a midwesterner's heart thump with envy.

Murrells Inlet was and is a place bursting with pride and respect for the power and bounty of the sea — a small enough community where people lean on one another to haul in oysters and make repairs after storms. And even though sometimes they would rather not, the locals all seem to know one another's business, even when things are supposed to be "hush-hush." Like one big extended family, but not always highly functional.

I had only read about places like Murrells Inlet — a world away from the Brookside of my youth. It's the kind of community where kids grow up with shucking knives in their hands and still address their elders as "sir" and "ma'am." Where the locals project an enviable spunk and swagger that comes from breathing the briny sea air, pulling in crab pots, gutting fish, and riding out hurricanes. A place where the English language sounds melodic and creative and drips off tongues like thick, sweet sorghum. Where a day described as "warm" anywhere else becomes "hotter than the hinges of hell." Where some of the speech comes alive with expletives like *damn* or a two-syllable *she-it*, which often fall clumsily into sentences where they don't quite fit. As in, "He knows he damn well better let me borrow damn money any damn time I want, or I'll beat the she-it out of him." And it's the sort of place where, in a pre-civil-rights kind of way, some white people might assume you agreed with their convictions and lean in close to whisper racial epithets that you'd never think of uttering.

IT'S ANYBODY'S GUESS as to how and when Frank arrived in Murrells Inlet. But based upon his personality and the scant details from the police report, this is likely how it went down:

Frank rolled into town on Saturday, June 12, 1982, looking for a place to crash. He turned off the two-lane Ocean Highway at the south end of town in his silver 1978 Plymouth Horizon and onto the main drag. A large wooden sign welcomed him to the SEAFOOD CAPITAL OF SOUTH CAROLINA.

As a nature lover, he surely felt the allure of the bountiful marsh-lands teeming with birds and the beauty of the densely wooded coastal forest of pine, palmetto, and live oak strewn with mint-green Spanish moss. He noticed — and likely scoffed at — the pastel and neon collection of high-priced seafood restaurants with wide wrap-around decks offering creek views and crowded all-you-can-eat buffet joints with large wraparound parking lots. He was the kind of guy who was drawn to the mom-and-pop fish markets and little oyster shacks where you could get a dozen oysters for a few bucks.

As the brackish humidity wafted through his window and teased his long black hair, Frank would have sensed something else. Some-thing subtle, yet palpable. Something he'd felt before, like the comfort of a favorite blanket. He would have smiled and nodded knowingly as he breathed in the town's unmistakable transience and the promise of its anonymity.

The warm air and fresh sea breeze surely renewed his hope and confidence. He craved a place like this where no one knew his past and where he could be whoever he wanted to be. This just might have been the perfect place to find a new family of fringe-dwellers he could relate to — young folks who worked the restaurants and bars during the tourist season and who liked to drink some beer and smoke a little weed. People who were out for a dose of adventure in their lives and who would accept his peculiarities.

He found a clearing in a strip of dense woods in the land between Highway 17 and Business 17, just south and west of the Admiral's Flagship restaurant, where he unrolled his sleeping bag and gath-ered kindling for a fire. It was a quiet spot about forty yards off the main road, lush with pines and oaks and little saplings with yellow-green leaves. A thick layer of dead vines and pine needles that smelled like a musty attic would have made for a soft forest bed. Occasional spots of hazy sunlight pushed through the nearly solid cast of clouds, illuminating the woods with a murky azure haze.

Frank might have found the spot on his own — he had a keen sense of adventure and an intuitive, inquisitive nature honed by years of hitchhiking across the West. But judging from its secluded location down a narrow path cut through the trees, it was **more** likely someone led him to the clearing. And it would have been just like Frank to pick up a local hitchhiker or pull over and ask the first person he saw for directions to a campsite. Since he would never think of hurting or taking advantage of anyone, he assumed that others would treat him the same.

As he cruised slowly up Business 17, Frank would have driven right past one of the most popular seafood restaurants in town, operated by one of its most nefarious residents.

chapter seven

Nance's Creek Front Restaurant still stands in its original location on the east side of Business 17, about a five-minute walk from where Frank's body was found. It retains institutional status in Murrells Inlet — like a loosely respected and reluctantly tolerated aging uncle to the other younger, hipper joints up the road. Although the family no longer owns the business, the restaurant still bears the Nance name.

As one of the last remaining fish-camp-style restaurants in the area, what it lacks in pretense and charisma it makes up for with endearing grit and decent food. The current building was constructed after Hurricane Hugo destroyed the original restaurant in 1989. Other than some fresh coats of paint and a new roof, not much has changed since then. An ample, unpaved parking lot with a few shade trees surrounds a tidy-looking one-story, blue-and-white building with a broad, covered porch offering a few wood rocking chairs and a welcoming blue-and-white awning. The interior retains its decades-old feel with long wood tables, wood paneling, acoustic tile ceiling, recessed fluorescent lighting, and busy dark commercial carpet. Large windows make up the whole back wall, looking out on an outdoor seating deck and providing a panoramic view of the Main Creek and the inlet beyond.

Nance's general manager, Pollyanna Milliken, made no apologies for the décor. "Back when seafood restaurants originated in the area, the focus wasn't so much on 'atmosphere' but delivering some of the best and freshest seafood possible — which we still do."

On that same spot in 1967, Paul Nance opened his oyster roast in a cinder-block building where his father stored bags of clams and oysters and distributed them to nearby restaurants and markets. Paul convinced his father to allow him to start roasting the oysters on-site and selling them from his storage building. As the oyster roast became more popular, the menu grew to include deviled crabs and boiled shrimp.

Paul expanded the seating area and added a porch to the building, and the space evolved into a full-service sit-down restaurant. It was a family business. His first wife, Cynthia, greeted customers at the reception desk and ran the register. His two daughters, Paula and Tina, and son Chris worked in the kitchen and waited tables. And in later years, Paul's sister Loraine was the restaurant's bookkeeper.

As the fleet of shell-fishing boats under Paul's direction grew, so did the reach of his seafood distribution and his narcotics empire, which meant more frequent spontaneous trips that weren't so mysterious to Cynthia. "Paul did his own thing. He had a lot of young guys working for him who would drive him places. They took a lot of trips to Florida and North Carolina. I stayed behind. It was business, but I knew he was going to have a big time."

At Paul's funeral, one of his employees, a guy simply known as Snakeman, told Cynthia that he once "sat on a cooler" for Paul as it was driven in a van up to North Carolina. He didn't say what was in the cooler, but Cynthia had her theories. "I suppose it was drugs or money or both."

Like a loyal gangster's moll, Cynthia benefited from her husband's increasingly nefarious activity and learned not to ask too many questions. "Paul would always tell me, 'What you don't know won't hurt you. So, I'm not going to tell you anything.' The less I knew, the better for him. I was ignorant to the point of stupid."

A former waitress who worked for Paul confided in me during a phone interview: "I can tell you this — Paul was a womanizer. He was known for running around on Cynthia. I'd describe Paul as a flamboyant jerk. He had a loud personality — always laughing and joking around. He was pretty nice to me, but his comments could be pretty rude. I wasn't afraid of him, but there was a certain ruthlessness about him. It seemed like all he cared about was money."

Perhaps no one had a better ringside seat to the greatest smackdown soap opera in Murrells Inlet than Craig Hair. For eighteen years he worked the front counter and register at Nance's restaurant.

"I was there through the divorces and all the fights and the gunshots and all that crap. It seems something was always happening around there. They were like rednecks with money. One night, Paul drug Mrs. Nance across the parking lot by her hair. He started shooting at customers who tried to stop him. He was high as a kite."

Paul's son, Chris, eventually stopped his father that night by beating him with a two-by-four. Their fight continued into their family home next to the restaurant. Customers heard gunshots coming from inside the house, so they called the police. Both Paul and Chris were arrested. Within two hours they were released and back at home.

Working in such a volatile environment was like a throwback to the 1800s. African American employees regularly referred to their boss as "Massa Paul." Craig felt like he had to walk on eggshells whenever Paul came around. "You'd never know what mood he'd be in. I don't know how many times I saw him walking through the restaurant with coke on his nose."

When Hurricane Hugo hit in 1989, Paul paid Craig to drive down to Florida and pick up his wife Cynthia from their Daytona Beach house. She wanted to get back and survey the damage to the restaurant. Craig arrived in the early afternoon to find an eager Cynthia, who was ready to get on the road. After a short rest, they drove the seven hours back to Murrells Inlet. "Well, Paul didn't think we'd be back the same day. And Cynthia caught him with his girlfriend in the upstairs bar of their house. That started the divorce. She was just tired of it at that point."

To this day Cynthia maintains that Paul was "handsome to the core," articulate, and formidable. He didn't take trash talk from anyone. "One night we were really busy, and this obnoxious guy kept trying to get in. Paul asked him to leave, and he wouldn't. Paul picked him up and threw him out the front door. Paul didn't know the guy had a fake leg, and it came off in the fight. Paul was just standing there with this leg in his hand."

By the early 1980s, Paul was worth an estimated $15 million. His restaurant was wildly popular and profitable, seating up to six hundred guests a night during tourist season, and his cocaine sales were booming. Nearly everybody in town knew about Paul's empire, but the police were never able to convict him. One summer evening in the mid-1980s, all twenty-seven of Paul's dealers were arrested in a well-coordinated sting operation. The intent was to nail the kingpin, but Paul was tipped off before it went down and was able to avoid being nabbed. Each dealer was held on $10,000 bond. Within twenty-four hours, Paul pulled together $270,000 in cash and bailed them all out.

His daughter Paula, who was nineteen and newly married, was swept up in that sting operation. Although she was not involved, she was present when a friend, who was wearing a wire, stopped by their house to ask her husband, Buddy, to pick up a "package," to which he agreed.

"They had nothing on me," Paula said years later. "Yes, I was on the tape, but I was in the background getting ready for work. I was talked into pleading guilty and got seven years, but it was reduced, and I served six months and six months' probation. I didn't put it all together until years later. They didn't want me, they wanted Daddy. The more I thought about it . . . Dang, he left me out to dry. He could have fixed it, but he didn't. It did change me. It made me not trust anybody."

According to Craig Hair, eventually Paul was convicted of tax evasion, fined $500,000, and ordered to perform two months of community service, which consisted of picking up trash at a nearby county campground. When the judge discovered that Paul was being chauffeured to the campground and was paying his employees to pick up trash for him, he gave Paul another month of community service.

To help raise some quick cash to pay his fine, Paul concocted a scheme to collect insurance money on one of his fishing boats — the

Tropic Queen. The next July 4th, Paul paid his nephew Donny Nance to anchor the boat near the jetties in the middle of the inlet's Main Creek and set it on fire. Donny dove off the side of the boat minutes before it exploded in a cinematic pyrotechnic display shooting flames fifty feet into the air. Locals still talk about it.

"Donny was dealing for Paul. He was shady," said a source close to the Nance family. "There's nothing he wouldn't do for Paul Nance."

An unapologetic flirt and a philanderer, Paul valued his family primarily as business assets. He took care of them and provided a comfortable lifestyle for them in order to maintain his facade as a family man and a reputable member of the business community. And perhaps no family member consumed more of his energy than his nephew Tommy McDowell, Loraine's boy. Loraine was Paul's favorite sister, and Tommy could do no wrong in Paul's eyes.

Many in town considered Tommy to be "touched" due to a tumultuous childhood in an unstable home. But Tommy was described by others, including his cousin Tina Nance, as an intelligent, charming kid who just misused his energies and talents. "He was genius level. Could have been anything he wanted to be. Could have been a millionaire if he'd directed his energy elsewhere."

Like a modern-day Fagan, the character from Charles Dickens's *Oliver Twist*, Tommy hung out with a group of younger boys who would go up to Myrtle Beach and bully the tourist kids out of their arcade money. Of course, Tommy always got a cut. And Tommy took other liberties with those boys, psychologically controlling them and, in some cases, sexually abusing them. Constantly seeking his next thrill and his next high, he experimented with drugs and developed a gambling addiction. He couldn't stay away from the video poker games that stood in some of the local businesses.

He often went to extremes to slake his insatiable lust for cash — writing bad checks, using stolen credit cards, stealing cars, and breaking into his neighbors' homes. One of Tommy's more lucrative hobbies was to take his father's deputy badge, jacket, and portable emergency light (Max McDowell was a sheriff's deputy in nearby Horry County), place it on the dashboard of his car, and pull people over on the highway to coerce money out of them. He also burglarized his uncle Paul's restaurant a couple of times, the last time breaking into the safe and stealing thousands of dollars. After that, Paul decided he'd covered for Tommy long enough and that the boy was just taking advantage of him, so Paul pressed charges. But at the pleading of his sister Loraine, he dropped all charges before going to trial.

By all accounts, Paul was verbally and physically abusive toward his only son, Chris, who grew up with his older cousin. Tommy was like a big brother who showed Chris the ropes of a hoodlum.

When I asked a longtime cook at Nance's restaurant about Tommy and Chris, he leaned close to me and squinted with a sparkle in his pale eyes, like a weathered ship captain. "Those boys were both dirtier that anything you got on the bottom of your shoes."

Bob Morris, former pastor of the Belin Memorial United Methodist Church in Murrells Inlet, knew Tommy and Chris and almost everybody else in that town. "Tommy was a mixed-up kid, but as nice a guy as you'd ever want to talk to," he said. "He'd sit right there in that chair and charm you all day long."

Morris said there was some speculation around town that Tommy, Chris, and two or three other local boys were trying to set themselves up as tough guys, so they took credit for a lot of the crimes that happened in town whether they were involved or not. He said some people around town heard Tommy bragging that he killed "the boy in the woods."

"I think Tommy McDowell didn't do it," said Morris. "But I think he capitalized on the situation."

Joey Howell had a different opinion. He was one of the two part-time sheriff's deputies patrolling Murrells Inlet back in 1982. He said, "I feel 100 percent sure that Tommy committed the murder. He was a known homosexual, and I believe that played a big part in it."

Howell theorizes that Tommy tried to sexually proposition Frank and a fight ensued. He had no evidence that such a scenario took place, just a feeling. Howell also said Tommy had a habit of reporting crimes he had committed. And Tommy was suspected of, but rarely charged with, committing many of the petty crimes in Murrells Inlet.

Much like an arsonist calling the fire department after setting a fire, Tommy would call the sheriff's office to report a crime, like shots being fired on one end of town. While the sheriff's deputy was investigating, Tommy would go to the other end of town and steal a car or break into a house or simply fire more shots just for fun.

Several months after Frank's murder, Howell picked up Tommy for some crime or another — he took Tommy in so many times for so many different things he couldn't remember why he was hauling him into the station that day. But this time was different. During the twenty-five-minute drive from Murrells Inlet down to the county jail in Georgetown, Howell talked with Tommy.

"Did you do it, Tommy?" Howell asked, referring to whatever crime he was bringing Tommy in for.

"Yeah, yeah I did," he answered very curtly and then proceeded with a detailed confession.

Howell pulled into the county jail parking lot and turned to face Tommy. "Well, since you're being so open and honest about everything, why don't you tell me what happened with the boy in the woods?"

Tommy broke down in the backseat of Howell's car and sobbed uncontrollably for half a minute and then gasped, "I ain't got nothin' to say about that."

Howell knew that a guy like Tommy wouldn't break down and cry if he didn't have something heavy on his mind. "It was totally out of character for him. Tommy was tough as nails."

And Tommy had a mean streak. Many of his high school mates, including Glenn Welch, avoided him. "I never went around Tommy McDowell. He was a cold individual. I was actually scared of him. I heard enough stories to know that I didn't want to be around him. If I saw him coming, I'd head the other way."

Another schoolmate who also grew up in Murrells Inlet had a different take. "Tommy was in my grade, but older than me. I wasn't afraid of him. He didn't like me 'cuz he knew I could beat him up. Tommy was more of a pedophile."

More than a couple of people I interviewed told me that Tommy had been fired from a job as a school bus driver in nearby Horry

County for molesting two boys. Not charged with a crime, only forbidden from ever working as a driver again. They intimated that Tommy's father, Max, with his influence as a Horry County sheriff's deputy, had something to do with shielding him from prosecution.

Tommy had also earned a reputation as a two-bit grifter. In 1987, he made a small purchase at a local pharmacy with a $10 bill. When the clerk gave him his change, Tommy claimed he had given her a $20. She knew Tommy and was wise to his incessant conniving. She didn't let him get away with it. She told him that when she cashed out at the end of her shift, she'd see if the till was off by $10. If so, she'd give him his change. Her drawer balanced out to the penny.

Tommy's disreputable deeds eventually caught up with him. He was nabbed and convicted in a check-kiting scheme that sent him to prison, where he died on September 26, 1994, from complications due to AIDS. In his waning days he lay weak and emaciated in a hospital bed, yet an armed officer was stationed outside his door, and he remained handcuffed to the bedrail. They considered him a "flight risk." Tommy's father had to plead with the prison guards to unchain his son so he could die with a shred of dignity. His mother, Loraine, buried Tommy, proclaiming his innocence in the murder of Frank McGonigle. To this day, she maintains that he wouldn't hurt anybody, not physically anyway. I interviewed Loraine on three separate occasions — on my first visit to Murrells Inlet in 1995, again in 1996 on a follow-up trip, and in the spring of 2019.

On my last visit, she solemnly greeted me as she held open the storm door of her tidy one-story home on the north side of town. What struck me immediately was the surprising youthful appearance of her skin. However, her smooth features and wispy, tastefully dyed hair could not mask her eighty years and the pain that seeped from her defeated, vacant eyes.

She ushered me into a dimly lit living room with the slow, determined movements of a woman exhausted by years of defeat and laden with shrouds of sorrow. I sat on the couch and scooted forward to steady my notebook on my knees. She sat opposite me in a well-worn armchair, yet her eyes never quite met mine, as if she were looking at my ear or the crest of my thinning hair. Despite her sadness, she sat up straight and dignified.

She seemed so fragile that I felt compelled to speak as calmly and softly as possible. "I know it must be hard for you to talk about something that happened so long ago. And I'm sensitive to the fact that this might dredge up some raw feelings."

"I understand. And it's okay. I want people to know the truth about Tommy."

"I'm sorry for your loss," I said. And I meant it.

"Thank you. And I have prayed for years that this case be solved, and my son vindicated. And really since my brother Paul died, our family has become so divided. Lots of nasty backstabbing and people trying to tarnish the images of both Paul and Tommy."

"A lot of people in town think Tommy was responsible for killing the boy in the woods."

"Oh, I know what they've said. I admit Tommy had problems and got into trouble, but he had a very gentle nature." She smiled faintly as her eyes drifted to some far-off place beyond her living room. "One year at Christmas, when he was a boy, he asked if we could cook up a dinner and bring plates to people who need them. He had a big heart."

"I spoke with your nephew Chris many years ago . . ."

"Chris?" She shook her head with disgust. "Chris spent years trying to change history by his version of what happened — just trying to diminish his role in the whole thing. Tommy couldn't even look at somebody dead, but Chris, he wouldn't miss a funeral; he was obsessed with death."

"Do you have a photo of Tommy you can show me?"

"Sure. I've got one in the other room." Loraine rose and padded softly across the carpet.

When she returned, she handed me a dusty four-by-six print of a lanky twenty-something man with light-brown hair parted in the middle and a well-groomed mustache, wearing large aviator-style glasses, seated on the edge of a recliner with his arm around a gray-haired woman.

"That's Tommy with his grandmother. They were very close."

Loraine sat back down and then leaned forward. She paused before speaking very softly and deliberately. "You know . . . my brother Paul knew about most things that went on in this town. And shortly before he died, he told me that Tommy couldn't have done it because he didn't have the nerve. He said, 'Loraine, I don't know exactly who killed that boy, but I want you to know that it wasn't Tommy.'"

I also spoke to Tommy's father, Max McDowell, on the phone, and he pled his son's innocence. "You know how people talk. I asked him about it once, and he said he didn't have nothing to do with it. He wasn't violent. He stole and stuff like that, but he always admitted what he done."

chapter eight

When I first approached Bill and Joan McGonigle about delving into the story of their son's disappearance and unsolved murder, I was nervous. I hadn't had a conversation with them longer than a few greetings at church or at their grocery store. And I hadn't seen them in years. They really didn't know me as an adult, as a professional, as a journalist. I suddenly felt the need to impress them as someone other than the Cosgroves' baby boy and Tom's little brother. I didn't want to come across as exploitative, so I proceeded lightly with empathy and balance. They, too, seemed a little uneasy.

I met them in the fall of 1994 at the townhome in South Kansas City where they retired after moving from their large Brookside house. After I exchanged an awkward hug with Joan and a bone-crunching handshake with Bill, we sat down at their kitchen table. "As you may know, I've been living in New Mexico for the past couple of years and writing for the *Albuquerque Journal*. I enrolled in grad school, and I'm interested in your story for my master's thesis. I'd like to focus not so much on what happened to Frank, but on your journey, your feelings. How did it affect your family? How did it change you? And how did it affect your relationship with your other children?"

Bill and Joan sat tight-lipped and nodded silently. Joan inhaled slowly as if summoning strength to recount their story as she had hundreds of times in the past thirteen years to friends and local media. They glanced sideways at each other with resolve. Joan looked like she was about to say something, but hesitated. Bill broke the ice with a warmth and directness that I didn't expect from such a formidable, stoic man.

"We understand." His words were gentle yet resonant with his deep butcher's voice. "And we really appreciate you asking us. There's a lot to tell."

I exhaled slowly. "Thank you. And I want to go at a pace you're comfortable with. As slowly as you need. I know this will dredge up a lot of feelings. And I want to be sensitive to that."

Bill nodded and then jumped right in. "I didn't always understand Frank, but I was familiar with his wanderlust. I was the same way at his age. So, when he didn't come home that first night, I didn't think much about it, except for the fact he rarely went out at night at all. But I figured, he was twenty-six and could take care of himself."

Joan sighed. "And besides, we were trying very hard not to meddle in his life. We didn't want to ask too many questions. He'd get so upset whenever he felt like we were prying, so we took a hands-off approach."

Frank often took off on spontaneous joyrides. He loved the road. No family, no expectations, no predetermined roles. And for better or for worse, being on the road meant he was moving — at least away from his gloomy thoughts and perhaps toward a better emotional space.

"Before he bought that used Plymouth," Bill said, "he drove around in a beat-up Volkswagen that had a screwdriver for an ignition key. And when that was out of commission, he got around by using his thumb."

But when two and then three days went by without a word from Frank, the McGonigles began to worry. Frank usually called to let them know where he was. And his siblings didn't have a clue where he might have gone. Mike remembered that Frank hadn't bothered to unpack the car after the two returned from their California trip a few days before. "He left his clothes stuffed into a duffel bag in the backseat. His sleeping bag, golf clubs, and tennis racket were in the trunk, and my boom box was still plugged into the lighter."

After a few days, working on a hunch, Bill called Frank's bank. He explained to one of the officers that his son hadn't come home and asked if he could check to see if there was any activity on Frank's account. The officer told Bill that Frank had withdrawn all his $3,800 and had tried to get traveler's checks.

Bill felt the first sting of many lost opportunities. "If he had gotten those checks, we'd have found him earlier."

At first, Bill was kind of glad when Frank left home. Almost everyone in the family would say the same thing. They were happy he had finally taken some initiative to venture out on his own and make his own way. His depression was finally showing signs of lifting, and he appeared to be getting better. But when Bill discovered that Frank had withdrawn all his money, he became suspicious. He took it as a sign that Frank didn't intend his absence to be a temporary thing, so he phoned the police.

Right from the start, Bill encountered nothing but cool bureaucrats in the missing persons division of the Kansas City Missouri Police Department. "The first officer I spoke to — I'll never forget his name, it was Trollope — he told me there simply was nothing the police could do for us."

No report could be filed because Frank was an adult, seemingly competent when he left home, and there had been no sign of foul play. It would be an invasion of Frank's privacy, he told Bill. "Ever since then, I've had the impression that the KC Police Department has an overinflated image of themselves. They're not terribly public-minded or very friendly."

This was the McGonigles' first glimpse of the lonely road they would travel to find Frank. This would be their first in a string of rejections from law enforcement organizations. The next few weeks were heart wrenching, mainly for Joan. Bill was concerned, but his pragmatic nature kept him emotionally distant. Joan went down to the police station in person and essentially begged them to help her, trying to convince them that something had gone wrong. "I told them Frank was the type of son who would know that his mother was concerned about him, who cared about his family. But without any evidence of foul play, there was nothing they could do to help us."

One day on the way out of the station, Joan saw a poster of a missing child in the lobby and jotted down the contact number. She called and spoke to a woman in California whose son was missing and who had started an organization to help other parents in similar situations. "She suggested I send out flyers and get friends to help me call authorities in different states."

The McGonigles also put out word along their extensive network of family, friends, and parishioners — a far-flung web of midwestern Irish Catholics they called the Catholic Ghetto. Everyone along the line seemed to know somebody who knew somebody who might know something, but so far nobody knew anything.

And everybody had their own theories about where Frank was and what he was doing. Many of the McGonigle kids remember denying the fact that he might be dead. His sister Joanie thought maybe somebody stole his car, since he regularly left the keys in the ignition. "He knew perfectly well there were nasty people in the world, and you couldn't pull the wool over his eyes easily. It's just that he didn't care. He didn't bother people, and he figured that people wouldn't bother him. He was a very nice person, a very gentle person."

She also thought that maybe he got robbed and was so down about getting all his money stolen that he just couldn't come back and face the family. "He knew he would have come back to a whole rash of shit from the family. And I don't know many people, unless they're from a big family, who understand how that could be."

A few of Frank's siblings simultaneously concluded that Frank had killed himself or put himself in a position where somebody did it for him — but they didn't dare share that pessimistic view with one another. His brother Billy remembers when Frank and Mike made their trip to California and stayed with him for a few days. "Frank really hit it off with an old guy named Lucky who lived in a trailer on my property. They spent hours together philosophizing about life and death. Apparently Lucky told Frank that it was honorable to commit suicide. When I heard what Lucky told Frank, I was furious. I said, 'Lucky, as far as I'm concerned, if you commit suicide, you're a cop-out and a chicken shit. And not only that, but if you commit suicide, I'll piss on your grave.' That was the last time I saw Lucky. He eventually did himself in."

"So, did you piss on his grave?" I asked.

Billy waved off the question. "Naw."

A LETTER ADDRESSED to Frank from the North Carolina Division of Motor Vehicles arrived at the McGonigle home in Kansas City on August 10. It was dated August 6, 1982 — almost two months after Frank left home. It was the only real clue the McGonigles would receive about Frank for the next nine years.

> Dear Sir:
>
> This is to advise we have received information from Chambers Servicenter, Wilmington, North Carolina, that the above vehicle was stored by Wilmington Police Department, Wilmington, North Carolina on June 18, 1982.
>
> If you have not already called for this vehicle, we would suggest that you contact the place of storage to ascertain condition of vehicle and release procedure.
>
> Yours very truly,
J. G. WILSON, DIRECTOR
>
> — Vehicle not in running condition.

Bill immediately called Chambers Servicenter and spoke to Earl Chambers, who told him they had towed the car in from the parking lot of a public housing project in a "rough" Wilmington neighborhood. Chambers said that some of the residents had called it in as suspicious, because it had been there for a few days. When he retrieved the car, the keys were in the ignition and there was a set of golf clubs and a tennis racket in the trunk. He had towed it to his lot and said he would store it there until the McGonigles picked it up.

"I knew Frank would no sooner part with that car than he would his life," Bill said. "And even if the old junker had finally broken down, Frank never would have left his golf clubs and tennis racket in the trunk."

Bill went back to the police with this new evidence of potential foul play. "I remember that Sergeant Trollope — I'm still just burned up over him. He said finding the car didn't prove anything. He said the car could have broken down there, or he could have sold it to someone or even lost it in a poker game. I think we should have been more persistent than we were; we trusted people too much."

Bill's son-in-law Roy Wiltrout, Joanie's first husband, was an officer with the police department in Kansas City, Kansas, not to be confused with the city of the same name in Missouri. The two cities share some regional affinities and midwestern characteristics, but little else, which causes perpetual, and often petty, territorial issues and rivalries. Roy confirmed that his counterparts across the state line were merely following procedure by not filing a report on a person who appeared to have left on his own accord. However, he said there were always exceptions. Roy sought advice from a co-worker in the department about Frank's case. The officer said he couldn't help because Frank was from Missouri. The only way they could investigate was if Frank had last been seen on the Kansas side of the line. Roy convinced the McGonigles to let him fudge a little on a missing persons report, saying that he was the last person to see Frank at his home in Kansas.

Roy filed a report on August 18, and the information was plugged into the National Crime Information Center (NCIC) computer to see if Frank had been pulled over for any violations anywhere or if there had been any unidentified bodies reported. Nothing turned up.

The following week, Bill and Joan loaded up their old maroon Plymouth van and headed east on Interstate 70 toward North Carolina to pick up Frank's car and tow it home. They never dreamed that Frank would go east, since he'd always traveled west and loved it. The most direct route from Kansas City to Wilmington is across Illinois and Kentucky, through Lexington, down through Charlotte, North Carolina, to the coast — about twelve hundred miles in all. Bill checked the mileage because he wanted to determine if Frank had traveled directly to the coast or had meandered somewhere else. Earl Chambers told Bill that the car's odometer read 49,794.6 miles when they picked it up. Frank had kept detailed records of the fiasco trip to California, including mileage, which he recorded as roughly 48,000 when they returned to Kansas City. So, Bill figured, if Frank had taken the most direct route to the North Carolina shore, there would still be 594 miles unaccounted for. Frank could have racked up those extra miles by meandering the back roads all the way, or by first going to someplace like Florida, then up the coast.

As Bill and Joan drove deep into the Piedmont area of the eastern United States, the forests grew dense, and soon they were driving along a four-lane highway that was merely a swath cut through dense pine, oak, and elm. Joan, who had never been in the area, was impressed by the beautiful green forests. "But those dark woods held something of an ominous feeling for me. Although I didn't say anything to Bill, I was thinking that Frank could be lying anywhere out there in those woods and nobody would ever find him. If you were to step only ten yards off the road into the trees, nobody would see you. It was a jungle. Frank could be anywhere, but I tried to push that thought out of my mind."

Bill McGonigle recalls how Captain Bloomer of the Wilmington police greeted them with compassion and cooperation. "He explained how officers found the car at Taylor Homes housing project, dusted for prints, and came up with nothing. The car was not in running condition, the keys were in the ignition, and the trunk was locked. He said the officers on the scene were very nervous when they opened the trunk."

Earl Chambers of Chambers Servicenter towed Frank's car to his lot at a charge of $45 plus a $4-per-day storage fee. After sixty-one days on his lot, the car had racked up a rent of $244. Bill also asked them to fix the car's distributor and regulator and to rebuild the starter, so it would be in working order when Frank returned home to get it. The final cost of picking up Frank's car, not including the cost of renting a trailer to bring it back to Kansas City, was $462.41. Bill was glad to pay it but was still unsettled by the fact that it had been found abandoned.

"We picked up his car and thought about looking around a little bit," said Bill. "He was at Wilmington — that's a seaport — and he'd always talked about going to work for the Merchant Marine or something. But we were in kind of a daze, and we were still thinking Frank was alive. You look back and wish you'd done this and wish you'd done that. But at the time we did the best that we knew."

Bill decided years later that they had made a mistake by not contacting the sheriffs in nearby New Hanover or Brunswick Counties. "Later we found out that when you get down to these southern towns, the police department really isn't much. The sheriff is the one that does everything. Our contact was with the police department, and we never did get involved with the sheriff. And that was probably our mistake because we didn't know better."

Although Bill held on to the hope of a miracle, he had a feeling then that Frank was dead. Bill thought maybe he'd picked up a hitchhiker and inadvertently flashed his money, and the hitchhiker had done him in, dumping his body in the woods. Or maybe Frank was in jail on drug charges and too afraid to let his parents know.

It was no secret that Frank smoked a lot of weed and had a penchant for LSD trips, so it was not out of the question that he could have been busted. Or, considering Frank's history of mental problems, Bill thought he might have had a mental breakdown and was in an institution someplace.

"You hear stories about people who have been gone for thirty, thirty-five years, and they show back up," he said. "You never know, and until you get positive proof, there's always hope."

When Joan and her husband returned to Kansas City, she enlisted the help of a friend who worked at the Kansas City Public Library, who compiled a list of all the counties within a 500-mile radius of Wilmington, along with the sheriffs, their phone numbers, and their addresses, including Georgetown County, South Carolina, which is about 109 miles to the south. Joan created a flyer with Frank's picture and all his vital information and prepared to send it to all the county sheriffs listed. But her inner circle of friends and the police convinced her not to waste time and money and wait for the national computer to do the work for her. So, they waited.

"If you can believe it, we went on nine years like that," said Joan. "We had a private detective for a while and put ads in the paper. I had a friend at the Social Security office check to see if there was activity on his account — whether he had gotten a job or not. And the Kansas City, Kansas, police would call every now and then to ask questions about what Frank was wearing or if he had scars or tattoos."

For years, the McGonigles and their friends fruitlessly searched for clues in the news items of various newspapers across the country. They kept a file with clips of hopeful articles like "Mother Finds Son After Starting a Search Network," and stories of interest like one from Wilmington, North Carolina, "Missourian Dies in Bike Accident."

Joan's brother-in-law Gus Huber helped as best he could by offering to hire a private detective and to buy some advertising space in various newspapers around the country — Kansas City and Columbia, Missouri; Wilmington, North Carolina; Reno, Nevada; Sacramento, California — places they figured he could have traveled through. The ad read, "Frank McGonigle or persons with information on his whereabouts call . . . Reward."

Gus also contacted a friend of his at the Social Security office to see if there had been a new address established for Frank. He wrote a short note to Frank that would have been sent on to him, if the people in the office had found him. "Dear Frank," the letter read. "Kindly call me collect. We all miss you. Love, Uncle Gus."

There were no responses to the newspaper advertisements, and the Social Security administration found no activity on Frank's account. Looking back at the string of frustrations and at the avenues taken and not taken, Joan could see where she went wrong. "We were just really dumb. When we had the idea about the flyers, we should have just done it. The ironic part of it is, I still have that list with sheriffs and counties on it — and Georgetown County was one of them. I can't get over that. All that time we were so close."

chapter nine

Three thousand, two hundred and eighty-five-days Joan McGonigle waited to hear some news about her son. And not one of those days went by that she didn't think of Frank, see his face, or recall his voice on the other end of the telephone line saying in his deep, gawky tone, "Hullo, Mom." Thousands of horrific images crowded her thoughts and dreams, some merely fleeting, others seeming to linger for hours while she cried or screamed to God in anger.

Joan and Bill dedicated many hours and days to praying and talking to God. On the seventh day of every month after Frank left, they arranged to have a mass celebrated at St. Peter's Church in Frank's honor. In the nine years, there were more than a hundred masses offered. And every year on June 7, the anniversary of Frank's departure, Bill and Joan asked all their children who were in town to come to the mass and then over to the house afterward for a family dinner.

But even at these annual reunions, Joan's kids really didn't talk much about Frank, at least not around her. She knows they were only trying to protect her from feeling sad. But she wishes they had asked her more often how things were going and had opened up about their own feelings.

A few years later, in her journal Joan wrote, "I only know my children by what they do or have done in their lives. There is not much sharing of their inmost thoughts and beliefs. Is that unusual for a parent and child? I feel they know me much better than I know them — I am a person who is pretty open and tell my feelings — maybe too much."

And she let her children know her feelings about Frank and about how his disappearance affected her. "You know, losing a child is just about the worst thing in the world," she'd say to them and anyone else who would listen. "I'd rather take on my kid's pain than to have anything bad happen to them."

Joan often found herself forcing the issue on her children, calling them with her own tears and fears. But many of the kids came to resent her emotional monopoly.

"After a while it sort of became her thing and her thing only," said Joanie. "She'd say, 'Well, you have no idea how it is to be the mother.' But on the other hand, she doesn't know what it was like to be the sister. Not to diminish her role, but siblings are just a lot closer to each other than to their parents. We had feelings about it all, too."

Mena said she tried to stay as distant from her mother's emotions as possible because she wanted to feel free to have her own emotions. "Her feelings could kind of take over. I'm not blaming her; that's just the way she was. Mom didn't want to give up control of feelings."

For Mena, it was difficult growing up in a home where she didn't know what her father felt. One of the closest moments Mena ever had with her father was when she was sitting by his hospital bed after his hip surgery, holding his hand.

"You know, Dad," she said softly. "A lot of times I've been kind of afraid of you."

"Why's that, honey?"

"Because a lot of times I don't know what you're thinking or feeling," she said.

After a short pause he answered, "Mena, neither do I."

"And to me, that was really revealing," she said.

With waves of uncontrollable sobs and cries of frustration, "Frank attacks" would creep up on Joan through the years and continued until her death in 2008. Once she was sitting in church, and she was just crying and sobbing when suddenly, it seemed, the Lord spoke to her: "You know, you put it in my hands, and you told me that you trust me."

"So that's what I attempted to do. I realized that life must go on, and I couldn't just sit there crying all the time. Some days I could do it and some days I couldn't."

Bill prayed that same way, and, as he let go, he began to feel in his heart that something bad had happened to Frank. Although he was frustrated with the police in Kansas City and in Wilmington, he realized that they had done what they could with the resources available at the time. And he understood that given limited jurisdictions, a sheriff may not be aware of something that has happened right across the state line or in the next county. Despite his frustration and times of anger, Bill remained emotionally stoic. Over the years he had become hardened to death, mainly because of his experiences in World War II where he saw many men around him die.

"I have a hard time crying at death because I don't think death is really that bad," Bill said almost apologetically. "I kind of think the good Lord was saving Frank from something."

As each of the McGonigles worked out their feelings and stripped away the layers of emotion, anger began to surface. "Before we found him and thought he was somewhere, and he wasn't calling, yes, there was much anger," said Bill. "But now I know that he never intended not to call us; he'd died about five days after he left home. He would have called us. I know it."

Also, there was anger building among the siblings for not allowing the true expression of feelings. And anger toward their mother and father for promoting an atmosphere of intolerance of differences. This caused both Joan and Bill to look closely at their past.

"If you take any one of your children, you could think of a lot of things you'd wished you'd done differently," said Joan. "So, I have kind of been going through that more than I was before. Just something I have to get through. I found flaws in my parents, so I tried to do differently, and I made other mistakes, and so my children see flaws in me."

Bill McGonigle, too, had a transformational revelation about his role in the family. He knew he did the best he could as a father, but this time of reflection caused him to do some serious thinking about how he raised his kids.

"I didn't spend that much time with them," Bill said with a bit of hesitation. "Except for with Billy, and I told him one time, 'If I spent as much time with each kid as I do with you, I could never go to work. I couldn't sleep. I couldn't eat.' A man doesn't get that much intimacy with his kids, especially with this large of a family." He paused and proceeded with caution. "Sometimes I wonder if the Catholic Church was right in promoting all of that."

Every vacation Bill and Joan took over those nine years, they looked for Frank, checked out hitchhikers on the side of the road, and scanned crowds. Twice they went to the vacation home of Joan's brother in Wrightsville Beach, North Carolina, which is a little more than a hundred miles north of Murrells Inlet. One year, while they were there at the beach, Joan saw two young men out in the ocean, and she was sure that one of them was Frank. She watched them closely for minutes, only to be disappointed when they came out of the surf.

Another time they saw a dark-haired man that looked like Frank driving a motorcycle traveling in the other direction. They turned the van around and followed him for miles before they could pass him and discover that he wasn't Frank.

Not only Bill and Joan but also the kids searched for Frank, especially at Grateful Dead shows. They thought that maybe Frank had joined the thousands of other Deadheads who faithfully followed the band year after year, show after show. It would be easy, they figured, to drop out of sight by doing that.

And there were dreams. Lots of Frank dreams. Nearly everyone in the family had one to share. Some of them believed their dreams were windows into another world — glimpses into a spirit realm. Others considered it a form of prayer, a way for God to speak to them when they were a captive audience. Either way, they were profound.

A few years after Frank disappeared, his mother dreamed about him on a Sunday morning. In the dream, Joan was sitting in a room somewhere and suddenly Frank was there. He walked over to her and put his arms around her, saying, "I don't want you to worry about me. I'm fine. I'm okay."

Then Joan woke up. As she rose from bed and began to dress for church, she felt a strange comfort come over her. When she got to church that morning, she broke into tears when she realized it was Pentecost Sunday, the day on the liturgical calendar (the seventh Sunday after Easter) when Christian churches celebrate the descent of the Holy Spirit upon Christ's disciples. Joan had been praying so much lately to the Holy Spirit that she interpreted her dream as a message that Frank was dead. And she was comforted.

Bill once dreamed he was at a Grateful Dead concert at Kansas City's former Kemper Arena, although he'd never seen the band in person, only in pictures. He was sitting high in the upper deck when he spotted his son Frank down on the floor. He shouted to Frank to stay where he was, and Bill fought his way through the crowd down to the floor, but when he got there, Frank was gone. He looked everywhere and could not find him.

Joanie was jolted awake out of a deep sleep one night a few years after Frank left. She was terrified when she woke that night because she was shaking, and her bed was literally, physically shaking and she felt immediately that Frank's spirit was present there and had woken her up like he was trying to get hold of her and shake her to say, *This is what happened. This is what happened.*

"Where are you? Please," she pleaded into the darkness. There was no reply.

Joanie realized then how deep her belief in spiritual beings was. If she was to believe in the saints and angels of her Catholic upbringing, then she had to believe that Frank's spirit was not at rest and was still there trying to let his family know what had happened to him. "I believe spirits are out there," she said. "They can intervene and talk to us."

After the family found out that Frank was murdered, Joanie and Renee compared notes about their experiences through the years. They discovered that their frequent dreams about Frank seemed to subside after about five years. They thought that maybe they had simply gotten used to the fact that he was gone and were not as upset about it. But when they discovered that Frank's body had been laid to rest after spending five years in a morgue, they wanted to believe that the dreams tapered off because his spirit was finally at rest.

In addition to various dreams about Frank, Renee had a spiritual experience in 1985 that reinforced her intuition that Frank was dead. She was living in San Francisco and ducked into a nearby Catholic church. Although she had not been attending mass regularly, she felt an overwhelming urge to pay a midweek visit. She slid into one of the pews and looked up to see three statues situated side by side on the same wood base. She immediately burst into a fit of uncontrollable tears. Not usually one to show her emotions, Renee sobbed as she looked upon the figures of St. Francis, St. Joseph, and St. Patrick — all three hewn out of the same piece of wood. She was overwhelmed with thoughts of her little brother, whose given name was Francis Joseph and who had chosen Patrick as his confirmation name. She knew then that Frank was not coming back, but she was somehow reassured that he was safe.

Although Frank's brother Mark was not a big believer in psychic powers, he felt something strange once when he was meditating at his parents' home during a summer visit. He was alone in the house that morning, so he took advantage of the quiet to meditate and pray for a couple of hours in his room. When he finished, he was in a rather peaceful, centered state, and he descended the front stairs and walked through the family room on his way to the kitchen. He suddenly noticed a picture of Frank that his mother had framed and hung on the family room wall.

"As I walked through the room, it was like this life energy just jumped through the picture, and I got this tremendous feeling of well-being. I just kind of swallowed that and said, 'Okay, I can live with that.' I knew then he was dead."

Mark's wife, Peggy, had her own encounter, although she had never met Frank. He disappeared long before she started dating Mark. Since she entered the family, she had heard many stories about Frank and seen many photographs. One picture in particular will forever remain etched in her mind. It was the same picture that Joan and Bill had framed and displayed in the family room of the house on Walnut Street — the one Mark had said many years earlier had seemed to emit an energy that leaped out at him.

Peggy often looked at the photograph of Frank and from it formed her own idea of his personality. It was taken at Mena's wedding in San Francisco the fall before he disappeared. His hair was tousled, and he wore a wrinkled khaki suit; a red, white, and black checkered shirt; and a red knit tie. A pink carnation was pinned to his left lapel, and he was sporting his patented half smile — the kind where only the left side of his face was creased with a hint of happiness. Peggy always thought he looked peaceful at the moment the camera caught his image, with a wall of green leaves just out of focus in the background.

Peggy said she finally met Frank one night in a dream.

"In my dream, there was Frank, looking just like he did in the picture. We were outside, and there were green, leafy trees around. I was really surprised to see him.

"'Are you Frank?' I asked him.

"He said, 'Yes.'

"Then I said, 'I thought you had gone away.' He said, 'I had, but I'm back now.'

"He was very peaceful and had a real sweet smile on his face. The feeling I got was that he was sort of saying, *I goofed. I wish I hadn't, and I'm back now. I've been away too long.*

"It was one of those really cool dreams where you wake up feeling like something really good just happened. I had finally met him. He had come to meet me and give me that message to pass along."

chapter ten

Frank had been dead for thirteen years when he first spoke to me. And I'm not going to lie — it was weird. I'd never engaged in an actual conversation with a dead person, other than regular pleas to St. Anthony to find my car keys and attempts to reach my deceased father. But neither talked back.

Frank's words came to me on a slow-motion summer morning in 1995. I lay flopped on my couch, my head sandwiched between two lumpy throw pillows. I had surrendered to frustration that had piled up like a mound of dirty laundry, accumulated over weeks of writing in circles. Endless rabbit-hole research. False starts. Manic proliferation followed by arid patches of squat. From my pathetic pit of despair, I recalled a suggestion my mother made earlier in the week. "Just ask Frank to guide you." She was spiritual like that.

So, I lobbed a feeble-hearted request into the universe with a groan. "Hey, Frank. I need your help. What should I do?"

Water.

It was just a feeling at first. Not even a recognizable word, but a sense of the serenity and clarity you might feel looking out at the ocean or lying on a dock watching the ripples on a pond.

Water.

Nice. Calming. I felt the urge to hydrate. I rolled over, sat up, and grabbed the half-full glass of water that had been sitting on the coffee table since breakfast. I drew in a mouthful, held it for a second, and then swallowed it in two measured gulps. Satisfying.

I lay back down and closed my eyes.

Water. Get to water.

I inched up on my elbows. Looked around. Now I sensed words — wispy yet clear. Not "out-loud" clear, but distinctly "in-my-head" clear. I rubbed my temples and dropped back on the cushion. I thought it odd, but nothing more.

Get off the couch.

Okay, that was a little weird. But I dismissed it as just a fleeting thought, an out-of-the-blue inspiration — which I didn't disagree with. I definitely needed to get up and do something.

You need to get your ass off that couch.

This time I bolted up. "Huh? Do what?"

You heard me.

"Wait. Heard who?" I swung my legs over and sat up, shaking my head.

It's me. You asked for help.

I stood up and made a lap around the coffee table. I frantically rubbed my fingers through my hair. "Okay, now I'm crazy."

No, you're not. Did you forget what the nuns taught you? Ask and you shall receive.

"I don't know what the hell is going on, but I didn't ask to hear voices in my head." I felt the absurdity of talking to myself.

Yes. In fact, you did. About two minutes ago.

I laughed and continued pacing. "Ah, this is what happens when I get too deep into my head. I just have to get some fresh air or . . . just curl back up and take a nap."

Nope. Now get out and find some water.

"Seriously?"

Dead serious.

I paused in my madness and put my hands on my hips with a kind of resignation that arises from the sticky residue of desperation. "Uh . . . Okay . . . I'll play along. I might as well talk to a dead guy. Sure. Nothing unstable about that. What kind of water? A creek? A stream? There's a pond at the park."

Nope. Big water.

"Hmmm . . . big water's hard to come by around here — unless the Missouri River counts."

Drive south.

"Uh-huh. You mean, now? Today?"

No time like the present. It's not like you've got anything else planned.

"Well . . . you got me there."

I looked over at my backpack discarded on the floor near the front door. I did have an old dog-eared road atlas in there. I supposed it wouldn't be totally mad to check it out and just see if there happened to be "big water" nearby. I fished it out, opened it, and scanned the map for blue splotches south of Kansas City. "There's a lake about an hour away. Pomona Lake. Looks pretty big to me."

That'll do. Get there.

If I had done weirder things, I couldn't recall. But at that point, a trip to a lake on a sunny day sounded as sane as anything.

It was a steamy, sticky, ninety-something-degree August afternoon. I packed a granola bar, a box of crackers, and a few bottles of water, slid into my sandals, and hopped into my red Nissan pickup with busted air-conditioning. I shoved aside a pile of CDs and cassettes and set a small open cooler next to me in the center of the bench seat where I rested my arm in a bed of ice. At least one part of my body would stay cool.

I backed out of the driveway. Windows down, warm air blasting from dusty vents. I hit the brakes. "Wait. This is certifiably nuts. Can't we do this from the comfort of my couch?"

Not gonna work. Just drive.

"Fine, but what's your deal with water?"

It's not for me. I'm dead. This is all for you.

Frank's words now seemed to be streaming to me more definitively and clearly, as if he were sitting next to me. Didn't even startle me anymore. Just seemed natural. His voice lilted — super relaxed like he was slightly stoned or had just woken from a long nap.

You're stressed, man. You need to get away. You need to remember the thrill of a spontaneous road trip. And besides, water soothes the soul. It's life giving. Necessary for creation. And you need a serious jolt in the creation department.

"Can't argue with that."

*Man, I used to do this all the time. Just take off and drive. It's how I
escaped. At least one of the more positive, less destructive ways I escaped.*

I popped a cassette into the car stereo. Side two of Grateful Dead's
American Beauty. Some of Frank's favorite music. The song "Truckin'"
came on midstream, right at the part where Bob Weir and Jerry Garcia
sing about a strange trip. Indeed. It had already been a strange trip,
and I sensed that Frank and I were just getting started.

"Nice touch. I assume you picked this one."

Of course. It pretty much sums up my life . . . and death.

I turned up the volume to drown out the wind with lyrics about
scratching the itch to bust out of the door and travel only to end up
longing for the solace of home.

Yup, that was me . . .

"Why the obsession with the Grateful Dead?"

*They're travelers, man. And most people can relate. They don't pull
punches about life. They're not afraid to talk about the hard times and the
good times. It's not pessimistic. It's just realistic.*

For the next hour I sang out loud with a dead man to my limited
collection of Dead music as I sped down Interstate 35 before turning
west at Ottawa. My T-shirt was soaked by the time I turned into the
entrance of the state park on the shores of Pomona Lake. I slipped a
folded five-dollar bill into the slot at the pay station and headed
toward the water glistening beyond the trees.

I parked near the boat ramp and stretched as soon as I stepped
out. Some high clouds had rolled in, taking the edge off the heat. A
warm breeze brought in a familiar fishy-marshy smell of lake water
that triggered a memory. Family vacations at the Lake of the Ozarks.
My siblings and cousins and I fishing for crappie from the dock,
arguing about who got to use the nice Zebco reel. As the youngest, I
got stuck with an old bamboo pole. We were all cranky in our
scratchy, mildewy, sweat-stained orange life jackets. "Is this why
you brought me here? To remind me of that?"

*Well, that's part of it, but you're getting ahead of yourself. Quit
whinin' and get down to the water.*

Flat boulders the size of sofa cushions were scattered along the
shore. I hop-stepped from one to the other until I found a slanted

rock where I could stretch out and dangle my feet into a few inches of tepid water. My back muscles relaxed into the warmth of the surprisingly comfortable sandstone slab. I closed my eyes and listened to the hypnotic lapping of the water against the rocks.

"Okay, Frank. Here we are. I found you some water. Now, what do you want me to do?"

Well, aside from taking a break and enjoying the lake, I want you to stay curious, keep digging, and keep writing.

"But why me? I didn't even really know you when I was growing up. You were nine years older than me."

Yeah, yeah, but I knew you'd understand. You know my family. And you're from a big family yourself. You get the dynamics and how emotions run high. And I know you can do it. It had to be you. You were chosen.

"By who? You?"

Well, yeah, but its bigger than that. It's . . . you know, God, the Universe, Source Energy, whatever you want to call it.

I rolled my eyes and chuckle-snorted. "Please. Seriously, why?"

Things will be a lot easier if you quit asking why. And remember, you asked me to help you on this deal. I been tryin' to guide you for months. Droppin' hints left and right. But you quit, man. You gave up.

"It got hard."

Well, you're the one who makes it hard. You keep banging your head against the wall because you think it's supposed to be hard. It's not. It's supposed to be easy. Gently down the stream and all that. It's a dream. I know it's a hard concept to grasp, but when you're dead like me, you'll get it.

I sat up on the rock, scooted to the edge, and stepped into the water up to my knees. The slippery rocks cooled my aching feet. Soothing. Healing. Just like Frank said. "So, what would you like me to say?"

Just tell my story, man.

chapter eleven

Guilt can be a debilitating force that exponentially grows as it feeds on itself. In a family as large and as Catholic and as Irish as the McGonigles, a tremendous amount of remorse can build up over time. Immediately after Frank left and in the nearly a decade of uncertainty that followed, they couldn't help but ask themselves, "What did we do to drive him away?"

To begin to answer that, his brothers and sisters decided they had to understand more about their family dynamics and about Frank's tenuous role within their clan.

The McGonigles are a group of very well-educated, highly intuitive people. "Perhaps too smart for our own good," said Mike.

They have the collective gift of intensely analytical minds that often are mistaken for cynical. They can look at what they would call regular world problems, regular world situations — social traditions, hype, fanaticism — and see them for their emptiness. Frank looked at the world through those same analytical eyes. He was a deep thinker who looked beyond the obvious and saw people climbing social ladders and career ladders and hurting others along the way and decided that wasn't for him. He knew that if he had to or if he wanted to, he could get by in the world, but he chose not to.

"Instead of analyzing something and seeing the good stuff in it, he analyzed it and saw the negative side to it and said, 'That's bullshit.' Instead of using that analysis to fit into a situation, he used it to be distanced from the situation," Mike said. "Some of us decide at some point in our lives, 'Okay, we'll play the game as much as we can.' And some of us decide never to play the game, and I think that's what Frank did."

As Frank grew older and more analytical, so did his unique brand of humor — dry, sarcastic, and cynical. At family gatherings, he sat on the sidelines flinging witty barbs and whispering insightful observations with ironic twists. Frank was smart — he loved writing and reading, especially about history — but he was lazy. He would try to work his younger brothers into the position of servitude by toying with their emotions.

"Get me a Coke," he used to tell Mark.

"Why don't you get it yourself?" Mark shot back.

Then Frank would turn up the guilt. "What's the matter? Don't you like me?"

Frank was particularly competitive with Mark, who remembers lots of football and hockey games ending with heated exchanges punctuated with pushing and shoving. Mark knew Frank really got fierce about winning, so sometimes he would let Frank beat him out of pity. With his older brother, Mark always felt some tension about who was taking care of whom.

Frank was known to upend board games if he didn't win. Possibly his biggest display of stubbornness and temper was what has been dubbed the Apple Jacks Incident. Bill and the boys took a camping trip to Padre Island, Texas, in the family's pop-up trailer tent when Frank was about nineteen. Jerry was usually the first one up and out of the tent in the morning. He'd poke around the campsite, light a fire, and start breakfast. On one such morning, Frank, who was still in his sleeping bag, hollered out to Jerry, "Dibs on the Apple Jacks." They had packed one of those variety packs of little cereal boxes along for the trip, and there was only one box of Apple Jacks. But Jerry had already poured out the highly coveted cereal into a bowl for himself.

"Too late," said Jerry. "I already poured them."

Frank lumbered out of the trailer in his underwear and saw Jerry about to pour milk on the cereal, so he grabbed the bowl. Jerry quickly grabbed the other side of the bowl, and they began pulling it back and forth.

Billy was sitting right there at the picnic table eating his own bowl of cereal when a devilish grin came over his face. With the flip of a backhand, Billy upended the bowl of Apple Jacks right out of his brothers' grips, launching little frosted O's into the air.

Frank was incensed and went after Billy, who never had a hard time handling his lanky, gangly little brother. They rolled around for a few minutes throwing some punches — Frank after blood and Billy merely humoring him. Frank stormed off and didn't come back for about four hours, but eventually they all laughed about it, and Frank and Billy went back to being friends.

Frank imitated Billy as much as he could. His major male role models were his older brother and his father. He was unlike either of them in most ways, but he tried to be like them — and that's where he began to struggle with his identity. Billy was a dominating figure who set the tone of male behavior. He was the family clown who stole cars in high school for fun, sneaked out past curfew, and was mean in his own way to his younger brothers. Some in the family think that Billy decided it was his job to make men out of Frank and the other boys — to rough them up a little bit, to challenge them.

"Billy used to beat the shit out of us all the time," said Jerry, like it was no big deal. "But the thing about him was, if you stood up to him, he'd usually back off. Billy was probably the best thing for Frank. Billy taught him how to survive."

Joanie described her brother Billy as very intelligent, probably with an IQ of 170, but someone who today might be labeled with attention deficit disorder (ADD), because he couldn't sit still in school.

"We come from a family of opinionated loudmouths," said Billy. "And I was the administrator of that. I had the older brother syndrome. I was cocky and probably made things a lot worse for Frank. I'm not proud of that."

As Jerry and Mark started high school, the McGonigle boys' foursome kind of broke up. As weekends approached, the discussions turned less and less from what mummy movie they were going to watch together to whom they were going to go out with and where. Jerry and Mark started making new friends and hanging out with them, not always including Frank. This was hard on their older brother because, as an adolescent, Frank had a hard time. He was never accepted by the other kids at Rockhurst High School, an all-boys Catholic school run by Jesuit priests.

He made it on to the varsity soccer team that went to the state tournament, although he spent most of his time on the bench. But it was still one the proudest accomplishments of his life. His mother now regrets that she never went to see one of his games — another source of guilt.

Frank had terrible, head-clogging allergies and bad acne, which didn't help his poor self-esteem. He never did anything socially in high school, never went to any dances or had a date. His sister Mena remembers working with Frank at the grocery store in high school.

Bill would keep the store open until seven thirty sometimes. One Friday night there were no customers in the store and Frank said to Mena, "Boy, I'd really like to go to the football game tonight."

"Go ask Dad; he won't care," said Mena.

"He'd just say no," Frank said, looking at the floor.

"Hey, Dad," Mena yelled to the back of the store where Bill was cleaning up the meat department. "Can Frank go the football game?"

"Yeah, sure he can go."

Mena had a hard time understanding Frank sometimes. "I didn't know if his pride kept him from doing things for himself or what his problem was. I felt like kicking him in the butt sometimes. I had little patience for his differences."

Jerry and his friends had an unspoken understanding about Frank and would often invite him to go out with them. "It was out of obligation, really, and my friends were cool with him."

But Frank rarely complained about anything, so his family never really knew he was upset until he would just burst into tears. "He had to have been really sensitive to be that way," said Mena. "Most of us recognized that sensitivity but were unsure about how to handle it. We knew it had to have been miserable to stay home every Friday and Saturday night in high school."

Frank always put up a good front and seemed happy, but they knew he wasn't. Joanie recalled visiting Frank in Columbia when he was a freshman at the University of Missouri. "I'd never seen him so happy in his life. He showed me around the dorm, and he seemed to have a lot of friends. Guys were coming in to say hi." Joanie slowly shook her head with a distant gaze in her eyes. "I remember being so happy for him."

Even though Frank was sensitive and gentle, unlike his boisterous, extroverted siblings, he was treated the same as everyone else. Nothing, it seemed, was sacred, especially a personality foible. In the McGonigle family, being different wasn't considered a good thing.

"Being from a big family tended to make us think with a herd mentality," said Joanie. Often factions formed on opposite sides of an issue, and there were times when a bunch of the kids would gang together and pick on one of their own. "We're just an Irish family. Poking fun, serving up a few shit sandwiches, and raking people over the coals was a way of life for us."

The kids inherited their knack for teasing from their father, who had always been a joker, poking good-natured fun at those he worked with, his customers, and his family. In the evenings, at the dinner table, Bill liked to challenge his kids intellectually. He would throw out random questions for discussion, like, "Do tea leaves float or sink?" Then he would facilitate a discussion by probing and questioning until sometimes an argument ensued.

"Dad joked a lot, so it kind of came down from him," said Mena. "Then my mom always wanted to be serious and have this Donna Reed type of family. So, we would make fun of her because of that."

Consequently, they rode one another hard about everything. "Sure, [Frank] teased and tormented and beat up on the other boys," said Joanie. "He was good at both giving and taking shit, but as he grew older, he became quieter, and his teasing never seemed as natural as it did coming from the others. It always seemed forced, like some uncomfortable survival tactic."

Frank would move about placidly and quietly for long periods, then suddenly somebody would push him too far and he'd explode. Like when he kicked in a door in the basement when he was fifteen. Mostly his anger would be triggered when people teased or hurt others.

"It was tough growing up in my family," said Billy. "There was a lot of peer pressure among everyone. If someone thought you were sweet on a gal or a guy, they would ride it till it fell. There was a pecking order, and Frank was at the bottom of what I call the first family. He caught a lot of flak."

Nicknames were popular with the McGonigles. Frank's siblings called him Fradinky, or Dinky for short, which he hated. His ears would turn red with embarrassment, and he would plead with his sisters to stop tormenting him. And later, after he broke his nose playing soccer, Billy called him Banana Nose.

Because Jerry had huge eyes and a huge head sitting atop a bony bit of a body, he was dubbed Skeleton Head or Mrs. Arms Eyes, after their elderly, sunken-eyed babysitter. They called Mark Señor One Brow. Mark was also known as Jerry's second body and Jerry was Mark's other mind. Mike earned the name Crab-a-lot, but most everyone called him Duggy.

Through all the teasing and joking and the skirting of emotions and sensitive issues, Frank somehow managed to effectively display his caring, intuitive self now and then. His love for his family often shone on birthdays and around Christmas when he offered thoughtful gifts. They were always appropriate and spot-on. Once Frank showed up unannounced at his sister Katie's door in Dallas at about four o'clock in the afternoon. It was the twelfth birthday of Katie's oldest son, Chris, who also was Frank's godson. Frank had driven all day from Kansas City to deliver a Jack London book to Chris in person. They sat and visited for about half an hour, when Katie insisted that Frank stay for dinner and for the night. "I can't stay," he said. "I have to get back in time for work in the morning."

Somewhere along the line, perhaps in college or as an effect of his drug use, Frank's sensitivity and cynical humor were magnified with a dark and introspective twist. He listened to heavy, depressing music and once told Mark, "What Jesus is to you, Neil Young is to me." And even the music in his head was dark. Once at a family party, Frank picked up one of his brother's guitars and started strumming the only two chords he knew. He strummed a G, then a C, back and forth, and he sang, "Waitin' to die, I'm just waitin' to die . . . "

Mark had watched Frank's steady decline for a few years and, assuming his savior role, wanted desperately to help Frank. Once when Mark was home from college for a visit, he found himself standing outside Frank's bedroom door trying to think of the right thing to say to help relieve his brother's despair. Mark agonized over the right words but finally went into the dark room totally unarmed, with nothing eloquent to offer. There were two twin beds, so Mark lay down on the empty one across from Frank. Not knowing what to say, Mark convinced himself that by simply being present he was helping his older brother.

"It got to the point that when I was around Frank, everything within me was silenced. Then suddenly a scripture verse popped into my head, but I didn't dare say it out loud. Frank wasn't too cool with anything remotely religious. So, I recited it over and over in my head — 'The Lord is close to the brokenhearted. Those who are crushed in spirit, He will save.' It was kind of like a feeling of, this man is suffering, and there's nothing I can do except be with him."

When they finally did speak, Mark asked, "Frank, what's up? Do you have any hope for yourself?"

"I do have hope, but it's too little too late."

"Well, I just want you to know that I'm here for you, if there's anything you need."

FRANK HAD ALWAYS been disorganized in just about every aspect of his life. The way he dressed, the way he kept his hair, even his diet made it seem like he was trying to look as bad as he could and that he didn't care what people thought about him. But Frank worried deeply about what people thought about him. Some in his family called it paranoia and linked it to his drug use. It was much more than that, though. He wanted so badly to fit in everywhere that he overanalyzed every comment that was made to him. And yet, he didn't seem to take any pains to try to present a better side.

In the last few years of his life, he generally looked rather squalid and unkempt. He would buy used shirts at the Salvation Army thrift store for a dime or a quarter and wear them for a couple of days and then throw them away, so he wouldn't have to do laundry. His black, wavy hair was almost always disheveled, combed only by the fingers he frequently ran through it. And near the end of his life, he rarely laughed and infrequently smiled, with a slight upturn of the left side of his mouth. Even in photographs his fixed, pensive brown eyes seemed to pierce the lens, as if he knew what was going on inside the camera or in the head of the photographer. His mother described him to police as walking with a shuffle, slouched over, and almost always with his hands in his pockets. He often wore a mustache and thin beard or goatee, which never looked like it was more than a week old.

His disheveled manner was just a surface reminder of his deeper apathy, lethargy, and general depression. His mother speculated that he felt like a failure, like he had not lived up to the McGonigle code of behavior and expectations. Like he was not a good example to his younger brothers, who began to leap-frog him in pursuit of education and the quest for careers. Frank had not quite completed the coursework for a bachelor's degree in history, although he spent six years at the University of Missouri. When he moved back home in the fall of 1980, he had no idea where he was headed.

"He told us that he'd experienced a nervous breakdown at school and decided to come back home," recalled Joan. "He just couldn't deal anymore. In fact, he thought maybe suicide wouldn't be a bad option. He was just a shell in those years."

For eighteen months he lived with his parents and worked at the grocery store. He'd come home in the evening, and he'd eat sometimes. Then he'd go upstairs and sit in his room with the lights off and the shades drawn and just vegetate. Mike smoked a little pot with him on occasion, more as a social thing than anything else, but, he said, Frank just seemed to have lost interest in talking to people or doing things.

Mike finally asked Frank one time, "What happened to you? What exactly is *the* deal?"

"Well, remember when they put Grandma Proof in the nursing home," said Frank, "and she went to hell and basically decided to quit living? Well, they broke her spirit, and I just feel like my spirit was broken."

Mike didn't know what to say in response.

"We used to hang out," Mike said. "I was dating a gal pretty seriously, so I had dates every weekend, but weeknights we'd hang out.
We'd do stuff. It was always a little bit forced. I was almost doing it
out of duty, because I knew that he needed somebody to talk to or to
be with. He knew I felt like that. It was a real weird situation. We
had good times together. There were times when it was really easy,
and there were other times when it was really forced. And there
were times when he was Frank, the person I grew up with, and
there were times when he was this weird spaceman who was just out
there, that didn't respond to you, that didn't have anything positive
to say. It didn't seem like he had anything to live for. Being that I was
at that age when I was having a blast, I went out on Friday and
Saturday night. Frank would stay home. You know he's twenty-six
and sitting home on Friday and Saturday night and I'm going out.
And you know I almost felt a little guilty about having friends and
having a good time because he didn't have either."

In those years, Mike was closer to Frank than perhaps anyone else
in the family, largely because he was the only sibling living at home
when Frank moved back in. When Mike graduated from high
school in 1981, he had his collegiate sights set on some small liberal
arts colleges in the Midwest and in Texas. He looked seriously at
following in the footsteps of his older brothers Mark and Jerry, who
attended the University of Dallas. But the situation at home bothered him. He saw Frank going through so many problems, and he
knew his parents felt ill equipped to help him.

Almost out of obligation to Frank, Mike stayed close and enrolled
at Central Missouri State University in Warrensburg, about fifty
miles southeast of Kansas City. He was worried about Frank and, as
the youngest in a large family often does, seemed to think he could
do something to make it all better.

Mike found his way home from college just about every other
weekend.

And sometimes Frank would hitchhike down to Warrensburg
for a visit. Mike often bummed a ride into the city on Friday afternoon to see his girlfriend over the weekend, hang around the house,

and visit Frank. Then Frank would drive him back to school on Sunday night, hang out and party with Mike and his friends for a while, and make it back in time for work at the store on Monday morning.

Those nights that Frank would drive Mike back to school were some of the closest bonding moments the brothers had. Sometimes the conversations scared Mike, because he would hear the bizarre things buzzing around in Frank's head when he let his guard down and was honest. Mike tried to sympathize with him, to be a good listener, and then tried to work his magic and say something profound that would bring Frank back "to the other side."

"It was obvious to everybody that Frank was having problems, and he knew that," Mike said later. "He was smart enough to know that people knew he was fucked up."

During one of those Sunday-night conversations, Frank told Mike, "Well, you know, my testimony wouldn't even be admissible in a court of law."

"What in the hell are you talking about?" Mike said.

"I read about this Supreme Court case that ruled that anyone who had taken LSD more than a certain number of times in their life was legally insane. So, I'm legally insane."

"No, Frank, you're not insane," Mike insisted, trying to encourage his brother.

"Hey, I know I've made some mistakes, and they're having a direct effect on my situation now."

Frank had dropped a lot of acid in college, and he was still having flashbacks up to the time he left home. Joanie said that sometimes when he was at work at the store she could tell when he was slipping into a flashback. "He would suddenly zone out and be completely blinded to what was going on around him. He once told me he was stocking the shelves and looked down at his shoes and found that he had lizard's feet. Of course, he freaked out, but he didn't want to make a scene, so he closed his eyes until his feet were normal again."

MIKE OFTEN COMPARED Frank's life to watching either a Greek tragedy, where everything seems ill fated from the very beginning, or a Jerry Lewis movie, where the plot and the pratfalls are outrageous and funny, but you just want to squirm and crawl under the table because you are so embarrassed for him. "And you just want to pick him up and say, *Don't be so stupid*. I just always thought that somehow through some magic I could say, *Frank, wake up!*"

One of those tragedies played out on a night when Mike threw a party for twenty-five or thirty friends when his parents were out of town. Usually when Mike entertained friends, Frank would wander down and say hello to everybody then retreat upstairs to his darkened room. But that night Frank came down and, while making his rounds, met two older sisters of one of Mike's friends, and one of them was particularly friendly to Frank — not flirtatious, just genuinely cordial. He noticed that Frank was having fun talking to her, and Mike could see the heartbreaking script unfolding. Frank was getting led on, hooked in, and Mike knew it was doomed because the girl was seriously dating another guy. And it wasn't as if he could say anything. He was just relieved to see that Frank was having a good time. Frank hung out and got drunk with the rest of the crowd until everyone was gone.

Even though he'd been up past three in the morning drinking, Frank was in unusually good spirits the next day at work — really happy, like when you've met somebody, and you're smitten, and you're feeling confident. "But then a couple days later I noticed a change," Mike said. "I knew Frank had called the girl and asked her out. Of course, she said no, she was practically engaged." Frank retreated to the solace of his darkened room with the door closed.

Sometimes Frank would be up all night pacing his dark room or walking the carpet down in the living room. When the flashbacks and the voices in his head reverberated at an unbearable pitch, he would rush to the living room, slip on the stereo headphones, and blast some Grateful Dead or Neil Young to dispel the demons.

Once his mother woke up in the middle of the night and found Frank stretched out in the empty bathtub with the light off. His behavior frightened her so much, but she didn't want to draw more attention to it. She wanted to help him without intruding on his privacy or embarrassing him.

Frank had no health insurance, so Bill and Joan offered to pay for him to get some counseling, if he was up to it. The first doctor he saw would send receipts home with the word DIAGNOSIS written boldly across the front. Once it said PARANOID-SCHIZOPHRENIC and another, MANIC-DEPRESSIVE.

"I can't believe a doctor would write something like that right on there for him to see," says Joan. "He was terribly sensitive to that sort of thing."

Joan and Bill found another doctor, one Frank could really relate to. Dr. William O'Connor had seen hundreds of patients, and Frank was just one of those people he genuinely liked — not as an interesting psychological subject, but as someone with whom he established mutual respect and understanding.

I met Dr. O'Connor many years later in his modest office just a few blocks from the McGonigles' Brookside home. By then he was fifty-something with thinning brown hair and gentle eyes that smiled through round glasses. He was folksy, simple, and could explain things in terms I could understand. And he refused to label Frank anything.

"I saw Frank for who he was — simply Frank. He was, in a sense, a little too good to live in this world. What happened to him is that he made a decision with, I think, his heart not to become a mean, aggressive person. But he had not figured out in his head how to do that and live in the world the way it was."

Dr. O'Connor quickly identified Frank's conundrum as an inability to identify with anybody else in his family. "He was not cut out to be like his father, who was obviously a lot different. And when he identified with some of his mother's gentler qualities, he obviously thought that was all well and good, but he couldn't grow up to be a mom. And he knew he wasn't like any of his sisters or brothers. Frank was simply a bit more unique. Perhaps if his parents had been traditional Amish farmers, he might have just fit into that culture a bit better."

The doctor compared Frank to the mythological character Perceval, who launched an epic quest for the Holy Grail. "Like Perceval, Frank wanted to be an innocent and gentle person, and he got that from his mother. And he wanted to be a knight, a successful male, and he got that from his father. But he could not figure out how to put the two together. So, he went off in search of that answer."

It's no secret Frank was angry with his family because he never fit in. Dr. O'Connor thinks Frank decided that the only way to solve his problem was to leave home, go far away, and break ties. That's what he did when he went away to college and stayed mired there for six years.

"What he tried to do was not care. I'm sure he didn't think this consciously," said Dr. O'Connor, "but it was like, *I'll go away, and I won't love my family, and I won't care if they love me, and that will take care of that*. I think what he found was that he couldn't do it."

When Frank experienced what he called a nervous breakdown, he asked his parents if he could move back home to see if he could get any closer to the answer he was searching for. After his months at home and sessions with Dr. O'Connor, Frank's spirits seemed to pick up, and his general depression was lifting just about the time he left. He seemed to be making progress. Bill, Joan, Mike, Joanie — really the whole family — thought that his covert decision to leave was simply the next step in his healing process. And perhaps it was.

JERRY MCGONIGLE AGREED with Dr. O'Connor's assessment that Frank was too good and too sensitive for this world. The Christmas after Frank moved back home, Jerry was on break from acting school in San Francisco, and Frank asked him if he would drive to Columbia to help him pack all his stuff and bring it home. Jerry agreed, and they drove down to the old grungy house Frank rented in Columbia and loaded the family van. They were supposed to get back that night to attend an annual family poker party, but Frank insisted on pulling over to satisfy his incredible sweet tooth with a piece of homemade pie at the little trucker café where he always stopped on his way home. They ended up sitting in there for hours as Frank told Jerry what he had been through psychologically. It became apparent that Frank had a very distorted view of things that his father and some of his brothers and sisters had said to him in his childhood. Similar things that were said to all of the kids, but because of what his family perceived to be hypersensitivity, Frank took as literally. Like that his father thought he was crazy.

"You remember when Dad said I was crazy?" he asked Jerry. "I was telling him about something that happened to me once and he said, 'Well, Frank, you're crazy.'"

"Frank, he didn't mean it literally," Jerry assured him. "He said that kind of thing to everybody. He didn't mean anything by it."

"Oh, yeah? He said it to me all the time and so did some of the others," Frank said.

Jerry knew better than to tell Frank that what he was perceiving was wrong. He thought it better to just listen and try to understand where Frank was coming from.

It was in that diner that Frank told Jerry about his two suicide attempts.

Once, Frank took a handgun with him down to the bank of the Missouri River right outside Columbia. He waded into the water up to his chest and held the gun to his head. He said he stood there for about two hours trying to convince himself to pull the trigger. His body would be swept away by the current and might never be found, he thought. But reason seized him, and he climbed back out of the river.

Another time Frank rented a hotel room in Columbia, turned on the gas furnace, blew out the pilot light, and just sat there. Right before he was about to pass out, Frank ran from the room. He just couldn't go through with it.

"It came down to Frank having a really strange sense of what a relationship was," said Jerry. "I think he was really in love with this one particular woman. She was friends with him, but nothing more. In fact, she was dating one of his buddies."

After he moved back to Kansas City and was living with his parents, Frank would occasionally drop in on his sister Joanie, who lived in town and was raising her own family. Frank was so withdrawn and unhappy that it wrenched her heart.

"What will I do? Where will I go?" he'd ask her in desperation.

"Frank, I don't know. But if you've got some loose ends down in Columbia, I'd go and tie them up," Joanie said, referring to the woman he really cared about. "Do you think that there's a possibility that she's staying with this other guy because she doesn't know how you feel about her?"

"Yes, it's possible," he said, hesitating.

"Well, go and find out, then decide," Joanie told him. To me, she continued, "I'm not sure whether he talked to that woman or not, but when he came back, he was almost in worse shape than before. And I thought, *Oh, my God, what did I do?*"

Joanie was not alone in her feeling that she had failed Frank. Jerry said that he knew Frank felt like he had let him down. Mena said the same thing. So did Mark and Mike. Drawn out over nine years, all the memories of Frank and how each member of the family treated him continued haunting them with a tremendous amount of guilt.

"I attribute a lot of the growth of the family to this having happened," said Joanie about Frank's disappearance. "The guilt and the regret start taking their toll on you and you have to start looking at other relationships and ask, *If someone else wanted to leave, would I be the one that would be responsible?* You've got to start forgiving, you've got to start listening, and you've got to quit holding these grudges. You have to forgive."

McGonigle Family, 1965. Frank is on the far right. (Courtesy of McGonigle Family)

Frank, 11 years old. (Courtesy of McGonigle Family)

The McGonigle men around 1975. (Courtesy of McGonigle Family)

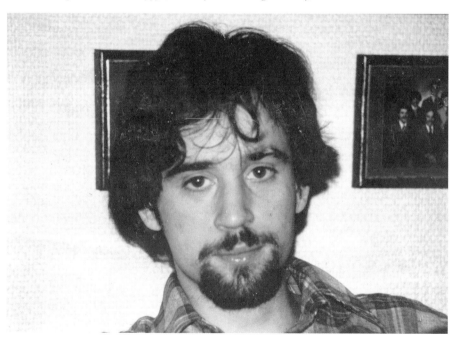
Frank, 23 years old. (Courtesy of McGonigle Family)

Tommy McDowell, Junior in high school, 1981.

Chris Nance, Freshman in high school, 1985.

Jeff McKenzie, 3rd grade, 1976.

Paul Nance, early 1980s. (Courtesy of Steve Strickland)

Chris and Paul Nance at a family wedding around 1980. (Courtesy of Craig Hair)

Bertie Nance, Paul Nance, and Loraine Nance, mid 1970s. (Courtesy of Paula Nance)

Bill and Mike at the family store, 2001. (Courtesy of McGonigle Family)

Georgetown County Sheriff's Department, 1980. Joey Howell is sixth from the left in the back row. Larry Hyman is far right in the back row. (Courtesy of Joey Howell)

The drawing by Frank's niece depicting Frank under the tree where he was found. (Courtesy of McGonigle Family)

Nance's Creekfront Restaurant. (Courtesy of Jim Cosgrove)

The author with Carol Williams at their reunion in 2019. (Courtesy of Jim Cosgrove)

The author, Mike McGonigle, and Tom Cosgrove during their visit in 2019. (Courtesy of Jim Cosgrove)

The statue of St. Francis dedicated to Frank in the courtyard at St. Peter's Church in Kansas City. (Courtesy of Jim Cosgrove)

Frank's grave with Mike's phone playing the Grateful Dead's "He's Gone." (Courtesy of Jim Cosgrove)

chapter twelve

In the law enforcement business, sometimes lingering cases get shuffled to a back burner to allow room for more pressing matters. But in Frank's case, he was relinquished to the fridge. Literally.

Because his was an open murder case, Frank's body remained in refrigeration in the Medical University of South Carolina morgue, just in case there were a trial and a need to identify the body or to conduct further tests.

The sheriff's investigation had fizzled. They had no witnesses, no weapon, no motive, no identification of the victim, and certainly no confession. Only hunches. With nearly all avenues dried up, it began to look like they were dealing with the random killing of a transient, perhaps rolled for what little money he may have been carrying or perhaps simply caught in the crossfire of the drug trade.

For the next few years, the only substantive activity in Frank's murder investigation was the forwarding of every .25-caliber pistol recovered from a crime scene in Georgetown County to the SLED labs in Columbia to determine if any one of them could be matched to the slug that killed Frank. There were about twenty-five guns in all. None matched.

An unlikely break surfaced in November 1986 when Georgetown County Coroner Mack Williams received a call from Dr. Conradi at the medical university. She was going through her records and noticed there had been no activity on case #08760 — the unidentified white male admitted back in 1982. She asked Mack if there had been any leads or inquiries about the body in the past four years. None on his end, but Mack said he'd check with the state SLED offices in Columbia on their progress.

Mack kept impressively detailed, typewritten notes, documenting every step and the dates and times at which he took them, like this one on Thursday, November 13, 1986, at 10:15 A.M. "I called SLED and was put in contact with Ms. Laurie Johnson in MPIC (Missing Persons Information Center). I asked her if the flyer had been placed nationwide and if there had been any results. Ms. Johnson said she knew nothing of the case but would check it out and get back to me."

Later that afternoon Laurie Johnson returned his call and said she had been through all the records and there was no indication that the case had ever been sent out on the national hotline. Mack felt a pang in his gut. He told Johnson that he would send her copies of everything in his files. She assured him that she would do everything she could to get the information out nationwide.

"The thought that the information on this boy never made it on the computer sickened me," Mack said years later. "Perhaps it had been misplaced or overlooked. I had heard that the national database automatically purged files after a certain number of years. Maybe that's what had happened."

Or maybe, he feared, he had dropped the ball.

Mack wasted no time in forwarding all the information to Johnson. With his official memo he added this personal aside: "Any assistance in identifying this body would be deeply appreciated. I know that somewhere there is a family wondering what has happened, and I'm sure that it would ease their minds somewhat if we were able to identify him and notify them."

For the next six months, Mack and the state investigators waited for a hit to come back from somewhere in the country. They checked the National Crime Information Center database weekly. There were no matches.

That's when Mack decided that Frank's body should be returned to Georgetown County and buried. But since he had never had to deal with an unidentified body before, he didn't know the protocol.

The attorney general's office informed him that Section 44-43-530 of the state code provides that any such "dead human body . . . is required to be buried at the public expense." Only two funeral homes in the county submitted bids for services. Johnson-Graham Funeral Home beat out Mayer Funeral Home, where Mack worked, with a low bid of $820.

On May 28, 1987, nearly five years after Frank had left his home in Kansas City, Mack accompanied a Georgetown County EMT driving a county van to the Medical University morgue in Charleston, about an hour south of Georgetown. The journey to retrieve Frank's body was more than just another duty that fell under Mack's jurisdiction. His presence and attention to detail were akin to a military honor guard escorting the body of an unknown soldier to a military cemetery.

It was nearly ninety degrees the day Frank was buried in Georgetown's Elmwood Cemetery across Highmarket Street from the Piggly Wiggly. Mack was eager to complete the burial early, as the forecast called for an afternoon thunderstorm.

When Mack told me this story, I could sense his anguish as he leaned forward with his forearms on his thighs, his fingers intertwined in a prayerful clasp. His tender humanity lay bare in the way he tilted his head and looked at me with pale watery eyes. He exuded dignity and honor as an elected official, as a father, and as someone who took seriously his role as a member of the human family.

"I had a kind of funny feeling about just taking this body out there and burying it with no services or anything," Mack said. "So, I talked to the minister from my church — I'm Presbyterian — and got him to go out there with us to say some prayers. Of course, at the time, I had no way of knowing that this boy was a devout Catholic."

Dr. William "Pete" Brown had been a close friend of Mack's for years and had always been impressed by Mack's humble nature. "He always treats everybody on equal footing, even those he doesn't know," Dr. Brown said. "So, I was pleased to help him out."

With heads bowed, Mack, Mr. Johnson (from the funeral home), Dr. Brown, and the backhoe operator stood beside the barren grave

— a $250 pauper's plot in the far southwest corner of the cemetery
— on that breezy day as the storm clouds rolled in from the west.

Dr. Brown thumbed through the golden-edged pages of his well-
worn Bible to the Book of Psalms and said, "Let us begin by reciting
a word from scripture. Psalm 90 asks the Lord to have pity on the
human condition":

> *Lord, you have been our dwelling place*
> *throughout all generations.*
> *Before the mountains were born*
> *or you brought forth the whole world,*
> *from everlasting to everlasting, you are God.*
> *You turn people back to dust,*
> *saying, "Return to dust, you mortals." (NIV)*

After a moment of silence Dr. Brown concluded by saying, "Let
us pray. Lord, everybody's presence on this earth is a gift from you.
So, we thank you for the gift of this man's life. And we thank you for
the contributions he made while he was in this life. On behalf of one
we did not know, we give you thanks, Lord. Amen."

"Thanks, Pete," Mack said, shaking his hand. "Appreciate you
comin' out."

As the men walked slowly to their cars waiting in the narrow-
paved drive, the backhoe operator fired up his machine and began to
fill in Frank's grave.

"It didn't really feel odd," said Dr. Brown, thinking about the
service years later. "But it just made me aware of how relatively little
we know about people — what shapes and what motivates a person.
To some degree we're all strangers to one another."

Although Georgetown County was only obligated to pay for
Frank's burial, Mack thought it only fitting that the grave be marked
with some kind of headstone. He convinced the county administrator to appropriate $79 for a white marble veteran's marker. The
inscription read:

WHITE MALE
DIED JUNE 1982
MURRELL'S INLET, S.C.

Years later, Bill and Joan McGonigle tried to reimburse the county for Frank's burial, but Mack told them it would require much more paperwork than it was worth. However, they did insist on repaying the $79 for the headstone, and Mack graciously accepted. He was, after all, a gentleman.

chapter thirteen

As was usual for Fridays, the meat counter at McGonigle's Market buzzed, and Mike McGonigle tossed another order of steaks on the scale. It was the second day of August 1991, and customers lined up in front of the counter waiting to place their weekend orders, grousing about the unbearable heat that had gripped the city. Outside the mercury inched its way up to the 105-degree mark, but inside the electric saw whined like a high-pitched dentist's drill as it shaved off pieces of dry ice, and the butchers hammered cleavers through slabs of ribs. The phone rang.

"Yo, Mike," shouted one of the store clerks over the racket. "The phone — it's for you."

Mike finished wrapping the order he had just weighed, slid it across the stainless-steel counter into the grip of a happy customer, and wiped his hands on his apron as he moved toward the phone behind the meat counter.

"Michael," came the voice from the other end of the line. "This is Detective Allen with the Kansas City, Kansas, Police Department."

"Yes, sir," said Mike, putting a finger in his other ear to shut out the noise. He recognized the name as the officer who had been in contact with his parents recently but thought it very peculiar that he'd call him at the store.

"I'm trying to locate your folks. I was wondering if you knew where they are."

"Well, yeah. I think they're out to lunch with some friends," Mike answered. He played it a bit coyly because he wanted as much information out of the detective as he could get. "I'd be glad to pass a message on to them. Is there something I can help you with?"

"Well, no. I really need to talk to them. Do you know where they went?"

"I think they said they were going over to Michael Forbes for lunch. You know, up there on 75th and Wornall."

"Do you think they'd mind if I called them up there?"

"No, I suppose not. Hey, is this about Frank? Did you find something out?" Mike asked excitedly, as his big brown eyes grew wider.

"I think it's best if it waits until I get the whole family together. I hope you understand," the detective said, trying to sound official yet compassionate. "I was hoping maybe we could meet tonight. If I don't catch them, please have them call me as soon as you can."

"Yeah, yeah sure."

"Thanks. Good-bye." Detective Allen hung up.

Mike stood with his forefinger on the hook of the phone, staring blankly at the floor thinking about his brother Frank and wondering if he was dead or alive. Whether, after all these years, some hunter had stumbled over his body in a patch of woods somewhere or he had ended up in a mental hospital with amnesia — the same scenes that had troubled his thoughts and his dreams for the past nine years.

"Hey, Joanie," he said, peeking around the corner into the office where his older sister was flipping through some catering orders. "That cop from KCK just called. I think he's got some news about Frank."

"Really? What did he say? I mean . . . is he alive?"

"He didn't say, but he's calling Mom and Dad over at Michael Forbes. Maybe we should head up there."

By this time, Mike and Joanie's brother Jerry poked his head in through the open office door. He was in town for a couple weeks of summer vacation from his teaching position at the University of West Virginia and had stopped by the store for some lunch. "What's up?"

"Detective Allen called looking for Mom and Dad. He sounded pretty eager to talk to them. I think he found Frank," said Mike.

"Well, what did he say? Did he tell you anything?" Jerry asked.

"No, I think he wants to wait until we're all together. Let's go find Mom and Dad." Mike untied his apron and tossed it on the back of a chair.

"I'm ready," Jerry said, inhaling the last bite of his sandwich.

"Me, too," said Joanie.

The three hopped up into Mike's pickup and drove the few blocks over to Mike Forbes's grill.

BILL MCGONIGLE AND his wife, Joan, were having lunch with the Reverend Vic Hummert, a Catholic priest friend of theirs, and another couple. They were in the middle of their meal when their waitress came to the table and said, "Excuse me, I have a phone call for the McGonigles."

"Who is it?" asked Bill.

The waitress answered, "It's a Detective Allen from the Kansas City police."

Bill's eyes darted and his lips tightened. "Joan, you'd better handle it." He often conceded communication matters to his wife, especially when it came to phones.

Joan was short and fiery with closely cropped gray hair and often wore wide plastic-framed glasses. And she almost always wore a smile supported by a nervous laugh. She padded quickly over to the bar to get the phone as her stomach churned. She'd been working with Detective Allen for the past few weeks to try to locate Frank and was eager for any news he could give her.

It was Allen who had contacted the McGonigles two months earlier and asked if he could reopen their son's missing persons case. He was a juvenile detective who was covering for a sick buddy in the missing persons division.

Allen was on the job a couple of days when he happened to be going through a file drawer and located six unsolved cases tucked in the back. Allen was granted permission to look into all six. He entered information about each into the National Crime Information Center (NCIC) computer to check if there were any arrest records or unidentified bodies that fit the descriptions. Within days, Allen had matches on four of the six, and they were alive. He was charged with a rush of adrenaline that he said was "like when you have your first baby and you sit there and look at it and say, 'God, I did this.' It's like taking a puzzle and putting it together and seeing everything fit in just perfectly."

Allen once helped a woman in Florida look for her son for several years. He'd call her a couple of times a month to update her and see if she'd heard anything. When he finally found the son living near her in Florida, the woman sent Allen a bunch of peaches as a token of appreciation. "I sure was pleased about that," he said.

The exciting part for him was bearing good news, but three of the four people he had located didn't want their families to know where they were. He was obligated to call the families and say he had found their relatives but couldn't tell them where they were. He could only say they were alive and didn't want to be contacted. He was heartbroken to deliver that kind of news. "I often wondered if it was worse to tell a family that their relative was dead, or alive and didn't want to talk to them. I know if I ever got that kind of message, it would devastate me."

But still, there were no matches on two of the cases — a woman and Frank.

As part of the procedure, Joan was asked to fill out a packet of information about Frank — his size, weight, birthmarks, scars, dental records, clothes he was wearing when he disappeared, and any other information that would be pertinent. Allen had called her several times over the past few weeks. One time he called asking for a fingerprint of any kind. The McGonigles were able to provide Allen with Frank's thumbprint from a chauffeur's license he used when he drove a school bus during college in Columbia, Missouri. Other times Allen would just ask a quick question about Frank, questions that seemed odd to Joan, but she figured it was police business.

Did he have any tattoos?

No, he had no tattoos.

What kind of belt was he wearing? Was it woven?

Yes, he did have a woven belt with a big eagle belt buckle.

Did he have KangaROOS running shoes?

Not sure.

In the past few days, Joan had spoken to Allen a few times and it seemed to her that he was closing in on a match. With each call he sounded more and more intense, and she figured something must have happened for him to call her over at the restaurant.

As Joan walked toward the phone at the bar, all the anxiety of the previous nine years welled up. The grief, the anger, and the guilt over what she must have done to drive Frank away rattled like a handful of nails in her belly. "I had prepared myself for this moment and told myself I could handle whatever the detective had to say. And it's awkward to admit, but I had gotten used to not knowing."

The thumping deep in her chest crept into her temples and made her almost dizzy as she reached for the phone. "Hello."

"Mrs. McGonigle, this is Detective Allen."

"Did you make a match? Did you find Frank's body?"

"Well, ma'am, I do have some information for you about a possible match, but I'd like to get the whole family together and tell everyone at once."

"Oh, I guess so," Joan breathed into the phone. She often said "Oh" out of exasperation or despair or for any number of expressions of other feelings. "Sure, when do you want to meet?"

"I'd like to come over there tonight," he said. "Can you gather everyone by tonight. I can make it a little later if you need time."

Joan thought about her kids all over the country and how she wanted them to be there with her. Jerry was already in town, so no need to worry about him. Renee was in California. Katie in Dallas. *Oh, Lord*, she thought, *how will they get here in time?*

"Would nine o'clock be all right, Mrs. McGonigle? And I can come to your house."

"Okay. I'll have everyone there. Oh, and Sergeant Allen," she said with a catch in her voice. "Thank you so much."

"You're very welcome, ma'am. Good-bye."

Joan almost dropped the receiver hanging it up. A hazy, dazed feeling filled her head as she walked back to the table.

"What is it, Joan?" asked Bill when she returned.

"I think he found Frank," she said quietly and slumped back into her chair.

As soon as the words slipped from her mouth, she looked up to see Mike, Joanie, and Jerry standing by the table. Joanie immediately went to her mother and hugged her.

"Mom, that detective called me over at the store . . ." started Mike.

"I just got off the phone with him," she said. "He wants to get together tonight. I guess we'd better call the other kids."

For Joan, the hours before Detective Allen arrived seemed as long as the nine years she vigilantly waited for her son's return. She had slogged through nearly a decade of nerve-frazzling mood swings and tissues full of stinging tears that would come unexpectedly. But she was never embarrassed by those tears, even when they poured in public. She wanted people to know. She wanted people to ask. She wanted people to feel the pain of jumping every time the phone rang, of hopefully wrapping Christmas gifts that would go unopened, of scanning crowds looking for Frank's black, curly hair, and of praying and bargaining with God for an answer.

NOBODY REMEMBERED MANY details from the night Detective Allen showed up at the McGonigle's house. Each member of the family retreated into their own self-absorbed fogs with their own fears and emotions to deal with. Nine years of anticipation and emotion had built up waiting for this moment, a moment they'd hoped would come, but at the same time dreaded. Nearly all the kids were able to get home by that evening; even Katie had flown in from Dallas. Only Renee and Mena were unable to make it. The pastor of their church, Father Jerry Waris, joined them. And other than those details, all Joan recalled about that night was Detective Allen, in his police uniform, delivering his message.

"As most of you know, I've been working with Joan and Bill for the past several weeks to try to determine the whereabouts of Frank," Allen began very matter-of-factly. "With the help of a thumbprint and dental records, we've made the positive identification of a body found in a small town in South Carolina as that of your son Frank. We are 99.9 percent sure it's him. The body was found on June 14, 1982, about a week after Frank left home. There was no identification on the body. And . . ." He paused and lowered his head, then looked back up to scan the faces in the room. "He had been shot . . . twice . . . in the head."

A gasp of sobs flooded the living room as the family began to embrace one another. The next several minutes were filled with a flurry of questions about how Frank was found, where he was, who was responsible for his death, what the police were doing to find the killer, why it took so long to make a match, why the police in Wilmington didn't figure it out since they were so close.

Although he didn't have all the answers, Detective Allen did his best to remain professional and explain what little he knew. He went through the story the Georgetown County Sheriff's Department had given him about how for years they tried everything they could to identify the body, and he told them how difficult it is for law enforcement agencies to doggedly pursue cases that are years old when agencies are short-staffed. He explained how simple things like not asking the right questions or not filling out the correct forms can send investigators heading in the wrong direction. He also told them Frank was buried there and how wonderful the sheriff's department and the county coroner's office in South Carolina had been in assisting him with the investigation. He patiently listened to everyone's concerns. He'd met with victims' families many times before and was well acquainted with the pain of such a message.

"I hated to go over there and tell them that their kid was dead," Allen said later. "But at the same time, I was honored to go over there. I knew I could finally tell them where their kid was. And at least they didn't have to die not knowing."

Allen explained about entering Frank's information in the national computer and getting ten potential matches. When he saw that one of them was from South Carolina, he consulted his atlas to find out exactly where Murrells Inlet was and its relation to where they'd found Frank's car in Wilmington, North Carolina. "Well, it's just right in that general area. And I thought, man, that's got to be him."

He contacted the sheriff's department in Georgetown and talked to their detectives and told them he had a thumbprint and dental records he wanted to forward. Within a day they came back with a positive match. The thorough dental records assured the identification.

After giving them a chance to calm down and get their thoughts together, Detective Allen took each of the family members, one by one, into the kitchen, where he questioned them about Frank and his habits and any possible motives for murder. The sheriff's department in Georgetown had requested that Allen question the family to see if there was any information that could help in their cold investigation.

During the interviews, Mike talked about Frank hitchhiking and what it was like to live with him for those months before he left. "He was not the same person I grew up with," he told Allen.

Billy said that he thought Frank had suicidal tendencies because once he had walked into Frank's room and there was a noose hanging from the light fixture on the ceiling. Frank was just lying there staring at it. "I thought he might have even offered somebody money to kill him," Billy told Detective Allen.

And when Allen questioned Jerry about Frank's sexual preferences, Jerry said he didn't think Frank was gay or anything, but he did remember Frank saying to him one time, "I think Dad thinks I'm gay." He was always painfully concerned about how others perceived him.

For Bill McGonigle, it was a bittersweet moment to find out that the waiting was over. In retrospect, he considers the years of uncertainty a blessing of sorts.

"I really feel that God spared us, even though we had to suffer," he said. "Maybe we needed all that time for it to come on us gradually. At first, we didn't dream of this, but then it wasn't a terrible shock."

That night as the family sat around the house trying to sort through emotions, Mike told his mother that if he had found out about Frank right away, the news would have destroyed him because of the tremendous guilt he had shouldered over the argument he had with his brother. "I discovered that time could heal wounds, even those that are self-inflicted."

For the next few days, the family stayed together at the home on Walnut Street and planned a funeral mass — a real celebration of Frank's life. And they had a chance to reminisce about Frank and about their family and about how hard it was growing up in a family that constantly teased. And again, the guilt began to well up in everyone.

"In many ways that line of thinking (the guilt) was destructive," said Joanie. "But then it became very positive because we started talking and finding out that other people in the family had their feelings hurt. I grew up with these people, but they're different from me, they have their own minds, their own likes and dislikes. And they don't have to be the same as me just because they grew up in the same family."

For the first time ever, Frank's brothers and sisters were able to sit down and talk to one another in a nonconfrontational way and reveal their innermost feelings without someone else jumping all over them, telling them they were wrong or making fun of them.

"It was like a miracle — it really was," said Mena. "Frank was the one in the family who carried the pain for our dysfunction. I really believe Frank's purpose in life was to do the things he's done for our family, to help us grow and to move on."

WITHIN DAYS, NEWSPAPERS throughout the Midwest and as far away as Phoenix and Cambria, California, ran the story of the McGonigles' nine-year saga. Even *USA Today* ran a short piece in its state coverage section. Joan was quoted in the article: "At least now we can cry and know what we're crying for."

As letters of sympathy poured in from friends and relatives all over the country, Bill and Joan were starting to piece together the details of what happened to Frank. They called the Georgetown County Sheriff's Department and spoke to a young detective named Bob Medlin, who was just new on the force when Frank was murdered and had been on the case for only a couple of years. Joan was relieved that Medlin was friendly and considerate. "Southern people have a lot of compassion," she said, almost as if she were trying to be polite.

Medlin told the McGonigles that there was a suspect, Tommy McDowell, whom they thought had probably committed the murder, but the department had little to go on. Medlin explained to them that the suspect was eighteen years old at the time of the murder and had a history of trouble with the law and that he was serving time in a state prison on another offense. About a year into Tommy's sentence, Medlin and a SLED agent had been at the prison to pick up another inmate, so they took the opportunity to question Tommy again, but they couldn't crack him.

The guards had called Tommy out of his cell that day to "meet some visitors." When Tommy saw who had come to call, the blood drained from his face, and, pointing to a white piece of paper Medlin had sticking out of his shirt pocket, he said, "Is that a warrant for my arrest for murder?"

"No, it isn't, Tommy," Medlin said. "But we would like to talk to you about that murder."

They commenced with the questioning, but Tommy denied everything. Medlin told Bill and Joan, "I know, I just know deep in my heart that it was him."

After speaking to Medlin and Mack Williams and discovering that Frank had been buried in Georgetown, there arose a dilemma about whether to bring Frank's body back to Kansas City. But when they heard that his body had been in the morgue for five years, the McGonigles decided it would be best not to disturb him again. It also would have been very expensive to bring Frank's body home, and, although Joan didn't want to appear to be materialistic, she realized that she still had other children, some living at home, who needed to be supported.

"Besides," said Joan, "that grave is not Frank. I think he's right here with us. I really believe that."

Still, Joan struggled with the decision, because she thought — just maybe — bringing Frank back to Kansas City would have helped her deal with her guilt.

"I think everybody goes through that grieving," she reasoned. "When somebody dies you have a body there and you see that they're gone — but to completely vanish out of your life — I'm having a hard time with that. But, you know, life goes on."

"The Lord has been very good to us by sparing us the need to go through a trial," Bill said. "I think that since that guy [Tommy McDowell] died of AIDS, he suffered a lot more than if they had put him in the gallows or the electric chair. He went to a higher court."

Joan agreed that harboring all that anger was nothing but self-destructive. "It's happened and there's nothing we can do to change it," she said. "And we can't let it affect our relationships with our other kids or with other people. You just have to go on."

chapter fourteen

The Catholic Church of St. Peter is a commanding English Gothic stone structure on the corner of Meyer Boulevard and Holmes Road in Kansas City. It comfortably seats about seven hundred people. On August 9, 1991, the night of Frank's memorial mass, hundreds more were left standing in the side aisles and spilling out through the two huge wooden doors at its entrance.

The nearly unbearable heat of the previous week had diminished to a pleasant seventy-two degrees by the start of the mass, and a light breeze was blowing through the open stained-glass windows of the church.

Frank's brothers Jerry and Mark and his two nephews from California planned a musical program for the memorial that Frank surely would have enjoyed, including a version of his all-time favorite Grateful Dead song, "Ripple." They began the gathering with a version of "I Am the Bread of Life," a contemporary Catholic funeral standby, the chorus of which concludes with, "I will raise him up on the last day."

Father Jerry Waris, the pastor of St. Peter's, presided over the mass. Joining him on the altar were Father Norman Rotert, the priest who was pastor of St. Peter's when Frank disappeared, and Bishop John Sullivan, the bishop of the Diocese of Kansas City–St. Joseph. After Father Rotert read the parable of the prodigal son from St. Luke's gospel, Father Waris stood before the throng to deliver his homily.

"A very special welcome to all of you who have come to recognize Joan and Bill and their family in nine years of wandering and nine years of searching and nine years of grief," he began. "Many of us probably walked into church tonight thinking we were going to attend a funeral and that we are to feel really sad. And we are, but if we know the hearts and aches of Bill and Joan and their children, their grief is over. Every month on the seventh day, they offered a mass that God would speak to them about what had happened to Frank. In a paradoxical way, their prayers have been answered. He was lost and is now found.

"Frank, like many, has died a terrible death. What is so sad, is that it is so commonplace — more and more each day. What pains you and us so much is that the very violence against which you've protested for so many years is that which took your son . . ."

Father Waris knew the McGonigle family very well; he had stood side by side with Joan and Bill at peace rallies and nuclear arms protests. He knew them to be peace-loving, spiritual people and knew that this sort of violence against one of their own must have enraged them deeply. But Bill often said that they didn't harbor much anger. He knew that whoever was responsible would be judged for it later.

"We'd never really had strong feelings against the person who did it because we didn't have him personified or have a picture or anything," Bill said. "But even at that, we have to move on and forgive."

Father Waris spoke about the biblical character of the prodigal son, who left his family, squandered his inheritance, fell into destitution, and made his way back home to ask his father's forgiveness. The father calls for a lavish banquet to celebrate the return of his son and puts rings on his fingers. An appropriate analogy because Frank just wanted to find his way home. Father Waris said the story is not only about a son who leaves home but also about a prodigal parent — defined as recklessly extravagant and generous.

"It's about the God of our fathers who, regardless of who we are, extravagantly welcomes us home. The last meeting, I believe, was not June 7, 1982, for I believe that the Lord of peace and God of justice, the Lord and savior of all, will call us home to the heavenly banquet."

After the sermon, Frank's dad made his way to the pulpit with the aid of a walker — he was recovering from hip surgery. "I want to welcome you all. I'm just overwhelmed. I feel very comforted that this many people would come here." Bill cleared his throat. "We want to thank everybody that's joined us in the remembrance of Frank at this time. It's been nine long years; we've been through some tough times. We've had a lot of miseries along that time thinking about what could have happened and what might have happened. But now we do know what happened. And although it was a bad death, we are relieved, and we thank God for all the people who helped us along the way. Support from the parishioners and the staff of St. Peter's, all our friends. We've received cards from people whom we do not know that took the time to send us a card because they felt so bad about Frank's death. There's an upside to almost every downside. The upside of Frank's death is that we are here to think about him. I'm sure if he knew this many people were going to come out, we'd never have been able to find him. He would have hidden someplace.

"We've met so many wonderful people on this journey. Sergeant Allen of Kansas City, Kansas, is not only a diligent detective, but he's also a compassionate man. When he finally got the news about Frank, he didn't call us up on the phone to say, *Your son's dead*, like a lot of police officers might have done. He said, 'Could you get your family together tonight? I want to talk to them.' At nine o'clock that night he came over and broke the news to us that it was a positive identification of Frank. He sat there, and he talked to us."

After a reception at the church, the McGonigles returned home, and for the next two evenings they sat together in their living room and had some difficult conversations, saying things to one another that had never been said. They talked about Frank and about their goals for the future and how their experiences had affected their lives. Frank's mother took detailed notes and shared them with me years later.

"My goal is to start the grieving process," said Mena, "by talking and sharing my feelings with others — to put it to rest somehow. I think we all need reconciliation and understanding."

"I agree," said Joanie. "You know, whatever happened, happened.

We'll never know exactly what our brother was all about. But what we can do is to recognize each person in the family for who they are and deal with it and not fall into the same traps we fell into before."

"What about you, Billy?" his mother asked.

"Well, I've got some deep anger at Frank. For years I thought that when he finally came home, I would just knock him out," he said, clenching his fists. "But sometimes I feel guilty, and I don't feel good about that."

"You know . . . when he left," Mike said, "his goal was to make us all feel terrible. I'm positive he left home because he had to, but he did not intend to be gone long."

Joanie interjected. "I think that's the key. He did not intend to leave for good. So, what do we do?"

"We have to remember," Renee added, "that there were so many factors affecting his mental state that were not our responsibility."

"I think we all have feelings of responsibility and guilt," Katie said.

"Mark, what about you?" his mother asked.

"When Frank left, I was really glad, but about four years after that, I barely thought of him. I could just rake myself over the coals for not thinking about him, but, you know, we all go our separate ways. For me to say good-bye to Frank, I need all of us to express our differences and feel connected with each other. Really, I've said good-bye to each person in this room. We're not the same. But now I want to find out about all of you. It's time to reconnect."

"I agree, we need to find some common ground," Billy said.

"Right," said Mark. "We need to shed our roles and labels and learn to be ourselves."

"You know, there was so much teasing as we were growing up," Mena said. "I think we need to start focusing on forgiveness."

"Or at least balance the teasing with affirmation," Mark said. "To affirm others by making fun of them is not normal."

"I never felt it was bad," said Billy.

"Oh, come on." Katie rolled her eyes in Billy's direction. "There were some really cruel things said. It certainly was not positive. And a lot of it came from you."

"It's kind of like a self-fulfilling prophecy," Mike added. "If you're teased about something for a long time, pretty soon you act that way."

Katie sighed. "I felt like I was surrounded by people who were constantly watching me and judging me."

Each member of the McGonigle family slowly, sheepishly nodded in agreement. And an unfamiliar yet inexorable pall of silence settled upon the room.

PART TWO

a touch
of gray

chapter fifteen

The day I met Carol Williams, I was stretched out in bed at the Prince Street Bed and Breakfast in Georgetown, South Carolina. It was February 1995 and I had a heating pad on my back, trying to work out the kinks of an already intense three days. The warmth emanating from the electric coils spread across my back like the way a good coat of suntan lotion feels after it's been sitting in the hot sand all day. The stress ticked away in twitches and spasms. And it wasn't as if I had done anything particularly physical in the previous three days, except drive twelve hundred miles and talk to a few folks about Frank McGonigle's murder.

Other than Nancy, the sweet, silver-haired owner of the B&B, I had been the only other soul in the house. The entire second floor of the place was mine — although I had chosen to limit myself to a comfortable room at the top of the stairs. The antique, four-post bed was the softest I had slept in for quite some time, and the assortment of antique crystal and porcelain dustables were certainly fancier than anything I was used to.

I had just slipped into the seductive hug of the queen-sized bed when the sound of a deep, horse-cackle laugh coming from the stairs jarred me like the peal of a telephone in the middle of the night. It started low and slow, a subterranean gut rumble, then gained momentum as it skipped up the gullet and erupted into echoes that slapped off the walls. A second, more diminutive voice tittered alongside the gut-laugher as two people summited the stairs and clacked across the hardwood floor into the room across the hall.

I squirmed deeper into the folds of the down comforter and pretended not to hear them. Maybe if I stomped over there and politely, yet firmly, reprimanded them for being so inconsiderate, they would feel awful enough to keep it down. But then, like a nagging old aunt tapping on my shoulder, guilt set in. It always happened to me that way.

You're in the South now, I told myself. And the southern thing to do, I conceded, would be to get up and greet my new neighbors. But the bed was so comfortable.

Eventually manners won out over spasming muscles. I took a few deep breaths, swung my feet over onto the floor, and padded across the hall in my socks. After affecting the most genteel smile I could muster, I poked my head into their open door. "Welcome," I said with strained enthusiasm and leaned my shoulder against the doorjamb.

A blond-haired woman, hunched over an open suitcase, looked up. "Hey there. We didn't wake you, did we?" Her voice lilted with the touch of a sweet, succulent drawl that made my heart skip with a flutter. I've always been a sucker for a southern accent.

"No, I was just resting," I said with a change of heart. "I'm Jim."

"Well, hi, Jim; I'm Mary Helen," she said offering me her hand.

"And I'm Carol," said a smiling woman who was sprawled out on the bed like a long slender cat. Both women looked fifteen or so years older than me. Maybe in their midforties.

Mary Helen took charge of the conversation. "What are you doing in bed at this time of the afternoon?"

"I pulled a muscle in my back yesterday. I was just resting it. No big deal."

She smiled and her eyes widened. "Come here. I'll show you a great exercise for your back." She plopped down on the floor cross-legged and began to stretch, then beckoned me to join her. "Come on. You try it."

"Well, all right." I shot a bewildered look at her friend, who smiled with an arched brow. I slowly slid down into the same position next to her and winced in pain as I mimicked her moves.

"It's really good for these muscles right here," Mary Helen said, running her hands in a fanning motion across my lower back.

Carol smiled from her perch on the bed. "Well, it's obvious by your lack of a rebel drawl that you are not from these parts."

"I'm from the Midwest . . . Kansas City," I said. As if that proud revelation meant something to southerners.

"Well, Kansas City. I hear they got some crazy little women there." Carol nearly sang the words to the old R&B classic. "Well, honey, why don't you have a seat here with us?" She patted the space on the bed next to her.

"I think I'll just stretch out right here on the floor, if you don't mind." I exhaled, slowly reclining onto the cool wood slats. "Are you two from around here?"

Mary Helen told me how she'd driven down to Georgetown from the Charlotte area to work on a documentary film for the Rice Museum about South Carolina's thriving nineteenth-century caviar industry. And Carol just tagged along for fun — needing a weekend away from her job as an office manager at a heating and cooling business.

"But that's not all she does," Mary Helen cooed, and the two chuckled.

"What? What's so funny?" I shrugged. "Did I miss something?"

"Well." Carol sighed with a dramatic pause. "I read charts and do horoscopes and things like that."

"Hmmm . . ." I raised my brows, which didn't help in containing my midwestern, show-me skepticism. "Kind of like a psychic or something."

"Something like that, but I despise that term," Carol said. "I prefer *energy reader*."

I had developed what I considered a healthy reservation about those who set themselves up as some sort of oracle, only to bilk money out of people and deceptively raise the hopes of desperate suckers.

"And she's good, too," Mary Helen said. "You remember that woman who drowned her two kids down here a few months ago?"

I nodded.

She was referring to the highly publicized case of Susan Smith, who, in October 1994, drowned her two sons, three-year-old Michael and fourteen-month-old Alexander, by strapping them into her car and letting it roll into a lake in Union, South Carolina.

"Well, Carol is the one that led the police to that lake where those kids were."

Part of me wanted to give her the benefit of the doubt. "But I heard that lady confessed and told the police where she'd drowned the kids."

"She did confess. But before that Carol told the police to look to the left of the boat ramp. And that's where they found the car. Besides, you think the police or the FBI are going to admit they used a psychic?"

"You mean, energy reader," I corrected.

Mary Helen rolled her eyes and flashed an annoyed smile. She had a confident, rapid-fire approach that began to inch closer to "in your face." Carol didn't seem to mind that Mary Helen was doing the talking for her. Carol's relaxed, peaceful demeanor balanced Mary Helen's amusing brashness.

I looked at Carol. "Tell me, how'd you know where those kids were?"

"She just saw it," Mary Helen answered. "The vision just came to her that night. It's not like she asked for it or anything. I was the one that convinced her to call the police down there. She didn't even want to say anything to them about it. Go ahead, tell him what happened."

Carol sat up on the bed and pulled her knees up close to her chest. "Well, I saw them there in my hall one day. Right outside my bedroom. I saw this angel holding two little boys. I thought, *How unusual that an angel should be holding two little boys in my hallway*. I didn't know the boys, but I looked at them closely, and suddenly I recognized them from the news. And they looked so happy and peaceful in the arms of that angel. I knew right then that they had to be dead. But I also knew that they were safe and happy."

"It really freaked her out," said Mary Helen. "When she called me, I told her she should try to look into it more and see if she could find out where they were."

"So, did you?" I asked.

Carol nodded. "I have what I call a vision crystal. I hold it in the palm of my hand and hold it to my chest and concentrate very hard. Immediately I saw two little boys struggling to get free from a car — the same two boys I saw with the angel. One of them was strapped in a car seat and trying to get out, and it was obvious that the car was under water. They were gasping for air — having a really hard time breathing.

"Now, I wanted to find out what body of water they were in. So, I concentrated a little harder and I saw an aerial view of a really long lake — not very wide — and a concrete boat ramp that runs down into the water. And the car was deep in the water off the end of that boat ramp."

I sat up and leaned against the bedroom wall.

"I didn't know what to make of it all," she continued. "But when I told a few people, they suggested that I call down there. So, I called the sheriff's department in the town and ended up talking to some guy from the FBI. And I told him that I was an astrologer calling from North Carolina. And he said, 'You're calling from area code 910,' and then he said my phone number. So, they had already traced the call. I guess that was so they could verify that I was telling the truth. I asked if they were taking information on the case.

"He said he'd take any information I could give him. So, I told him what I saw, and when I mentioned the long, narrow lake, he got real interested and asked me more details about that. And I knew that they had already checked that lake, so I told him, 'You have already looked where they are, but go back and look again. The car is in deep water and hung up in a tree about sixteen to eighteen feet to the left of the boat ramp.' Well, I had no idea at the time that the lake they were in was named Long Lake. The guy thanked me and hung up."

"The next day it came out on the news that they had found the kids," said Mary Helen. "I was so excited, I called Carol right away."

"My phone rang off the hook that day with calls to congratulate me," Carol said.

"The guy from the FBI even called her back and thanked her," said Mary Helen. "And he asked her if he could put her on his list of psychics, in case they needed her in the future."

"Seriously? They do that?" I asked.

Carol smiled and nodded. "The worst part about it, though, was that for the next day or so I had one of the worst asthma attacks I had experienced in a long time. I thought I was going to have to go to the hospital. You know sometimes when I expend that much energy on reading something, I actually take on the physical pain of those who suffered. Since those boys were gasping for air in the back of that car, I suffered from a lack of oxygen. I was wiped out for days.

"Anyway," she said, "tell us about you. What brings you to these parts?"

"I think my life's going to sound pretty boring after that." I chuckled and stretched out again on the floor.

"Oh, I get the feeling you lead a pretty interesting life," Carol winked. "So, darlin', something important brought you here. What was it?"

"A project," I said, purposely evading a more direct answer that surely would require hours of explanation.

"A project? Come on, you can do better than that. What line of work you in, honey?" Mary Helen prodded. "And don't tell me it's sales. I just despise salesmen."

"Don't we all have something to sell?" I asked with a cocked smile.

"Oh, don't pull that crap on me," Mary Helen laughed. "I just wanna know what it is you're sellin'." She wriggled around on the bed like a fidgety child.

"I'm a writer."

"A writer? What, like a reporter or something?" Mary Helen's voice squeaked with disappointment. "So, do you work for a newspaper?"

"I used to write for a paper in New Mexico. Now I'm doing some research for a book about a guy from Kansas City who was murdered down here about thirteen years ago."

Carol sat up and scooted to the edge of the bed. "Interesting."

"Yeah. He grew up in the same neighborhood as me. His family and my family were pretty tight."

Mary Helen, who was still sitting on the floor next to me, leaned in. "What happened?"

"How much time you got?" I asked. "It's a long story."

"We got all night, darlin'. And it sounds like maybe you and Carol should talk about this a little more," Mary Helen cooed with wide eyes. "You know, she might really be able to help you out on this."

"No, that's okay, really," I protested, although deep in my gut I sort of wondered what would happen if she took a psychic peek into the case. "Anyway, we better start getting ready . . . cocktail hour approaches."

Our hostess, Nancy Bazemore, was an energetic, party-loving, martini-sipping widow who had invited us to attend the opening of a photo exhibit that evening at the Rice Museum. As a warm-up, she insisted we join her and some friends in the parlor of the inn for some pre-show cocktails.

After limbering ourselves with some southern spirits, we walked the two blocks to the museum. Being strangers in town, Mary Helen, Carol, and I hung out together at a corner table in the exhibit gallery. We drank wine and made up gossipy stories about the locals. After the reception we decided to sample a little taste of Georgetown, maybe drop in somewhere for a bite to eat and some drinks. But finding a lively watering hole, even on a Friday night, proved to be about as difficult as finding a Democrat in all of Georgetown County. It being off-peak season, many of the eateries had GONE FISHING signs in the windows.

A friendly couple on the street directed us to Tucci's, Georgetown's Little Italy, a year-round local favorite where the southern hospitality flowed as easily as the margaritas with Grand Marnier. We laughed and drank shots of tequila. I told them the story of Frank's disappearance, and we drank some more. We hugged and sang and howled at the moon — literally. It was past two thirty the next morning before the three of us stumbled arm in arm through the back door of the bed-and-breakfast.

I SPENT NEARLY half the next day in bed. When I finally rolled out, I padded down the massive oak staircase and shuffled into the kitchen. I found our host, Nancy, at the stove, and Carol was sitting at the table working on a bowl of soup and a sandwich. "Mornin', ladies."

Nancy turned to greet me. "Well, well, look who finally decided to grace us with his presence. C'mon, sit down here and have some lunch. We got to get some color back in those cheeks."

I sat down across from Carol and smiled. "How you feelin'?"

"Like a cat used my tongue for a scratchin' post."

After I had a few spoons full of soup in my belly, I started to feel more human. Nancy asked how my research was coming.

"Pretty well, but I get the feeling there are a lot of secrets buried in this town."

Nancy laughed. "You got that right."

"Most people around here seem to agree that Tommy McDowell killed Frank," I said. "But I don't. I don't think he had the guts to pull it off. He was a troublemaker and a thug, but not a killer. I get the feeling there's someone else involved who's still alive. And I think there are a lot of tight-lipped people around here protecting him."

Carol, who had been listening intently, slowly put down her soup spoon, wiped her mouth with a napkin, looked at me calmly, and said, "You're right."

I tilted my head. "About which part?"

"All of it. There was a second person involved, and he's still living around here."

The skin on my neck and forearms tingled. "How do you know that?"

"I see it. I feel it," she said.

All I could think of to say was "Hmmm . . ." My journalist's brain was resisting, but my gut told me to consider what she was saying. "Look, psychic stuff is not really my deal, but would you be willing to help me with this story?"

"Darlin', there are no accidents. Our meeting was not a coincidence. And yes, I'm planning on helping you," she said with a coy bit of a chuckle. "But it's not only because you're asking me, it's because there's a higher energy working here, and it's asking me. Besides, once someone asks me to help, I can't refuse."

"Carol, I really appreciate this."

"Oh, I know you have your doubts about me, but before this whole thing is over, you'll experience a conversion. You'll be a believer, I guarantee it."

We agreed to meet later and drive the twenty miles up to the woods in Murrells Inlet where Frank was murdered.

chapter sixteen

A satiny mist covered the windshield as I steered my pickup onto the sandy shoulder that ran alongside the woods where Frank's body was found nearly thirteen years earlier. As we stepped out into the soggy high grass, the late afternoon was waning toward dusk on an overcast, dreary day. Carol rubbed her hands together. "Honey, this is gonna be good. You ready for this?"

I shoved my hands in my coat pocket and shrugged. "You know, I don't make a habit of hangin' out with psychics in the woods."

She playfully punched me on the shoulder. "I told you, I'm not a psychic."

"Right. Energy reader. Whatever."

Carol took one last drag on her cigarette and dropped it at her feet where it snuffed out with a hiss. "C'mon, let's go see what we can find out."

She tromped off through soggy underbrush that smelled like a mix of pine and wet dog. Although I had only known her for twenty-four hours, there was something about her I trusted. Instinctively I felt she knew what she was doing. I followed so closely I could see mist forming a delicate net of droplets on the curls of her auburn hair. She stepped between two trees, ducking nimbly under a low-hanging branch. My thirty-year-old legs were working hard to keep up with this forty-eight-year-old grandmother.

After a few yards, she froze among the thin-trunked trees and saplings and tilted her head. I nearly bumped into her. Her eyes closed. Her lips moved silently. I didn't know what to do. I didn't know if we were suddenly praying or summoning spirits or what.

Carol stumbled backward and fell into me. I was able to grab her under the arms to keep her from falling. She laughed. "Someone just shoved me."

"Who?" We were the only two there.

"I don't know. But it was playful. I was asking permission to open up the scene and follow the energy. I was seeking verification that the energy was present, and I was shoved. Kind of like someone saying, *Hey, I'm standing right here.*" Carol closed her eyes again and cupped her left hand, as if receiving something. The fingers of her right hand fluttered in a pushing-away motion.

"I see three people standing here," she whispered hurriedly with a cigarette-harsh southern accent. "What I see is . . . I see jeans, ripped here." She pointed to her knee. "Bleached, faded, old. I see tennis shoes. Um . . ." Her voice trailed off into an uncomfortably lengthy silence.

I was getting that antsy I-have-to-pee sensation I used to feel as a kid playing Hide and Seek. I could hear only the faint sound of cars passing on the wet road thirty yards away and drizzle dripping from the branches.

"One of them left. I don't know if the one who left is still alive." She paused again, her hands still moving. "He went to see Paul. Who's Paul?"

"Paul was the guy who owned the restaurant," I answered. "He's dead now. He used to run drugs . . ."

She waved her hand at me. "I see a shrimp boat, but it's not in the water. The name on the back of the boat is . . . *Ann* . . . something *Ann* . . . *Missy Ann*, maybe." She hesitated, then launched into a rapid-fire pace. "He knew about it. One of them went for pot. They had some . . . he went to buy pot . . . Frank pulled out the money."

"To pay for the pot?" I interjected as my heart pumped faster.

"He gave the boy the money for the pot. They told him he couldn't go along. He wanted to go. They told him no, that the guy wouldn't sell him the pot if . . . with Frank along the guy wouldn't deal with him. He was a stranger. He didn't deal with strangers — didn't trust them. Frank gave them his money."

"Frank wanted to go with them to get the pot?"

She nodded. "Yes, and he was disturbed about it. He did not have his money in his pocket. That's why I see the tennis shoe. He had his money in his shoe or his sock. He took his shoe off. Did he have both shoes on when they found him?"

"I don't know." Although I distinctly remembered seeing both shoes on him in the crime scene photos, but maybe one of them could have been untied.

"He took his shoe off for the money," she continued.

"So, one guy left to buy the pot . . . was he there when Frank was shot?"

"No," she said abruptly, as if she were trying to hush me up. "There was an awful lot of excitement. Fast heart . . . real fast heart. Perspiration. Trip. Duck . . . he went to the right." Carol's knees buckled, and she moved to her right as if dodging something.

This flurry of details was getting me amped up. I had spent months researching and investigating and developing my own theories about Frank's murder. What Carol saw was eerily close to how I had imagined it going down.

"The one who stayed behind killed Frank. He's a smaller fella. The one that stayed behind is shorter, the shorter of the three. He's a blond. A dirty blond. Real light brown, real dark blond. Bad teeth. The guy who pulled the trigger has no conscience at all, none. No conscience at all. No remorse. No guilt. He laughed. He laughed out loud."

"As he pulled the trigger?"

"He laughed about it when the other one came back. 'You should have seen his face when I shot him,' he said. The other guy came back with . . . they did prop him. They propped him against the tree. That's not how he fell. They propped him. Was the wound here?" She pointed to the middle of her forehead.

"No, one shot grazed his left temple" — I pointed — "and one in his left eye."

"There is a mark or something here." Again, she pointed to her forehead. "The pain wasn't in his eye. It was here. I see brilliant light, bright light. It was instant death. He was frightened. Fast heart, perspiration. He did not suffer. There was no great pain for him. There was one shot of pain. Pain and bright, white light. They took the car. The two of them took the car; they took the beer. They took the money. They took a boom box . . . The one who killed him took it. This guy still has his boom box. Did Frank leave home with a boom box?"

Although she didn't look my way, I sort of assumed she was talking to me, so I answered with a tentative strain, "Yes, I think it was in his car."

"Okay, but it wasn't in his car when they found it," she said confidently. "This guy took it, and he still has it."

Carol was on a roll. It was like she had slipped into some other dimension and was drinking in this information from a fire hose and trying to spew it back to me before she lost it.

"Then one of them handed Frank's wallet to the other and said, 'You have to be Frank.' Lots of movement. Lots of shuffling. Wait . . ." Carol paused. Her brows furrowed, and her lips tightened. "There's an energy here that pushes . . ." Her hands came up in a defensive posture.

"Dirty blond hair and brown eyes. An unusual combination to be brown-eyed and blond-headed. There's a tattoo. He put the tattoo on himself. It's not professional, really sloppy."

"The one with the blond hair has the tattoo?"

"Yes. The one with the boom box has the tattoo. There's a skull tattoo."

"Skull?"

"On the left arm," Carol said.

The muscles in her face relaxed. Her head tilted to one side, and her voice sounded softer, less anxious.

"Frank died but didn't leave here immediately. His spirit stayed . . . Total disbelief. He really didn't believe he was dead at first. He had a very difficult time with it. He was angry. Extremely angry. He was thinking, *How could they do this to me?*"

The scene Carol wove was so vivid, I could see it playing out right there among the trees. I was fascinated she could capture so much detail about an event that had happened nearly thirteen years earlier.

And her ability to feel Frank's emotions blew my little Catholic-schoolboy mind. Sure, I had been trained as a journalist to doubt, to question, to analyze, but for some reason I didn't question anything she was saying. I went with it. She didn't know Frank or his family or me. She lived more than a thousand miles from where we grew up in Kansas City. She knew nothing of this case, except for the few details I told her the day before.

"When Frank accepted what had happened, that he was dead, that's when he really wanted to go back to his family," Carol continued. "Tremendous bond to home. Tremendous anxiety about leaving. Not wanting to be here — wanting to be home. He . . . he felt really bad for someone in his family. The one that he had words with. Wanting to change the words, the angry words. Did he argue with someone before he left home?"

"Yes. His brother Mike. The two had a big blowout the day before Frank left, and both said some pretty harsh things."

"This brother probably took it harder than the rest. Very difficult for him. His brother should know that Frank loved him very much. He wants to comfort him and reassure him. He loved him very much . . ."

Carol started walking through the leaves and brush and stepped over a stump. "It's right back here . . . over here," she said, pointing.

"Can you see it?"

"I see flashes of going to the right. Falling back to the . . . moving quickly or falling off to the right side," she said, demonstrating the motion. "That's why they positioned him with his hand . . . when they found him, his legs were out in front of him, his left arm behind him. He didn't fall that way. That's not how he fell." She paused and thought for a second. "Was the car blue or black?"

"Kind of a light gray, silver," I said.

"Then they got into another car," she said, "another car that did not belong to them. After leaving here, they got into a dark car, an old Buick or Pontiac, an old junker. It wasn't theirs."

She paused and thrust her hands into her jacket pockets and surveyed the scene again. "That's it." She shrugged and then slowly shook her head as if reconsidering. "Except for the . . . the saddest part of all of this is the feeling for his brother — this sorrow for his brother."

"Yeah, and his brother took it pretty hard."

"He wanted to change the words. His heart traveled to the one he had words with. That regret that he couldn't change it, he'd never get to change it. He'd never know how much he truly loved him. Or how much he really meant to him. Did the brother have a premonition that something was going to happen to Frank? Was he scared for Frank?"

"Well, not him in particular. His whole family was very concerned about him."

"Someone was very scared for him," she insisted. "Someone in the family was really frightened for him. They were afraid that they weren't going to see him again. Maybe his . . . mother? She feared that he was never coming back."

Carol's head turned slowly, and her eyes scanned that long-ago scene. She slowly nodded. "That's it. That's all I've got."

The sky had grown a darker shade of gray, which made it more difficult for us to trudge out of the woods. Carol stumbled and snagged her stocking on a downed tree branch and tore a hole in it. She laughed. "You owe me a new pair of stockings."

When we climbed back into my truck, Carol started recalling some things she'd left out. She said sometimes she hears and sees things she doesn't think are important, so she doesn't vocalize them at first.

"I have to learn to say everything, because you never know what might be important to someone," she continued. "I've got some names: Paul, Fred, and Becky Ann or Missy Ann or something Ann. I don't know if they mean anything to you or not."

"*Missy Ann* was the name you saw on the boat, right? I haven't heard that name, but I'll check into it."

"Also, when the boys left, they drove north, past Myrtle Beach. They drove in two cars," she said quite assuredly.

"You know, they found Frank's car in the parking lot of a housing project in Wilmington, just across the North Carolina line."

"Sure, I know where that is." She nodded with widening eyes. "That's wild."

Since she was on a roll, I pressed her for more information. "Can you tell me more about the one who shot Frank."

"Those eyes," she shuddered. "They are so unusual. A light brown, almost tan, like the color of creamed coffee. And the tattoo was a faded blue, like he'd done it himself with a needle and some ink or some ashes. The kind you see guys do when they're trying to kill time in jail."

Then she seemed to snap out of her faraway gaze and said, "Usually things will come to me a day or two later. And when I get home, I'll get a reading from my vision crystal."

I exhaled slowly. "Wow, I've got a lot to process. And, Carol, I really appreciate this."

"Oh, it was nothing, darlin', really. Now you owe me dinner." She laughed. "Let's go eat."

chapter seventeen

Later that evening, I called Mike McGonigle at his home in Missouri. He had become my go-to contact in the family. Because of the history of friendship between our parents and siblings, we had an unspoken familial respect for each other. Although he made himself willingly accessible, and we had spent many hours together detailing Frank's life, we were not close, but we were growing on each other.

I told Mike about Carol and how she agreed to go with me to the woods. I took a deep breath and laid into a methodical replay of what she saw. I told him about the two guys with Frank in the clearing, Frank asking to buy some weed, the money in Frank's sock, the gun, the shots, the perpetrator's laughter, the moving of Frank's car, the boom box, and the tan-colored eyes. Mike listened. No interruptions. No questions. I paused for a moment when I got to the part about the argument he had with Frank. I told him how Frank wanted to go back home and change his harsh words. How he wanted to make things right with his brother.

"She said that the one he argued with should know that Frank loved him very much."

There was silence on the other end of the line until I heard a couple short gasps of air. "Man, you've got me all choked up."

"I'm sorry. I just thought you should know what happened. I mean, I don't know if you believe in this stuff, but most of the things she said were right on."

"No . . . no, I'm glad you called. I appreciate it. And . . . you know . . . she said something about a boom box. That boom box was mine. I left it in the car after our trip to California. I was really pissed that he took off with it. I don't know if this helps or not, but I had my Social Security number engraved on the back of it when I moved into the dorms my freshman year of college."

I hopped to my feet and started pacing. "Hell, this just might be the break we need. What brand was it?"

"It came from Radio Shack. A Realistic, I think."

A flurry of scenarios and conversations erupted in my brain. "Should I tell the guys at the sheriff's department about all this? I've been working with one of the detectives here all week, but he's going to think I'm crazy."

"If it helps, I believe what Carol told you. All the things she saw are exactly how I imagined it happened."

"Thanks. And I'll let you know if I come up with anything else."

Before he hung up, Mike's voice quivered again. "All right, take it easy."

I paced the kitchen of the bed-and-breakfast for the next hour. I was trying to make sense of it all and trying to decide who to tell and how much. I needed some feedback from the outside, so I called my mother. She was a grounded, spiritual person generally open to metaphysical weirdness and might offer some sound advice. She listened patiently and said, "You have to take what Carol told you as the truth, and do what you can to make that truth be known." She paused. "Jim, please be careful."

She wasn't the only person that week who hoisted the flags of caution. After I had interviewed the Reverend Bob Morris, the pastor of the Duncan Methodist Church, he firmly shook my hand as I was leaving and said, "It was a pleasure meeting you. And Jim . . ." He followed with a brief but dramatic pause. "Be careful."

Mack Williams recommended caution. Bob Medlin and others at the sheriff's department hinted at the peril of disturbing the proverbial hornet's nest. And even Nancy, the owner of the bed-and-breakfast, appealed to my common sense. "Honey, remember people do things differently around here."

I lit out early the next morning for Murrells Inlet fueled by a breakfast of eggs, grits, and coffee at the Thomas Café in Georgetown. I had compiled a list of about ten people to talk to that day, including follow-up interviews with Chris Nance and some of the employees over at his family's restaurant.

I drove back and forth along the two-mile stretch of the Inlet's main drag about seven times, ducking down many of the dozens of sandy side roads, checking people off my list as I tracked them down and asked them a few questions. By early afternoon, I was tired but eager to reach the bottom of my list. One name left — Jeff McKenzie. He had grown up in the area, not far from where Tommy McDowell's grandmother lived near the edge of the woods, and ran around with Tommy and the other kids who lived along Business 17. I turned down a road marred with pits and cracks in the blacktop and was inching along slowly, checking house numbers and names on mailboxes, when I spotted a shrimp boat on an empty lot surrounded by a chain-link fence. It was up on blocks and had a FOR SALE sign tacked to its port side. Painted in large black letters on the boat's transom was MISS ANNA. This had to be the boat that Carol saw in her vision the previous day — the one with a name like *Becky Ann* or *Missy Ann*. And right across the road was the home of Jeff McKenzie. I pulled into the gravel driveway and walked the path to the door of a weathered pale-blue trailer.

A shriveled, gray-stubbled man wearing overalls and a fishing cap answered the door.

"What can I do for ya?" he mumbled in a low Carolina drawl.

"I'm looking for Jeff. I was told he lives here."

"That's my son," he grumbled and shot me a skeptical squint. "Whacha need him for anyhow?"

"I'm working on a story about a guy who was killed in the woods over here back in '82. I thought he might be able to help me out."

"He don't know nothin' 'bout that," he said, slowly pulling the storm door back toward him.

"Right, right," I protested. "I just thought he could give me some insight as to what the town was like back then. You know, some local color."

"Well," he said with resignation, "he's out in the crick gatherin' oysters. He'll be back when the tide comes in. You'll find him in a shack down there by the wata behind Nance's restaurant."

"I'll try to catch up with him. Thanks."

I parked my truck under the shade of a live oak in a rutted, sandy drive that ran beside Nance's restaurant. The oyster shack the old man had mentioned was about twenty yards away. I reclined back in my seat, resting as I kept an eye on the place — a small, whitewashed wooden building with a pitched roof and ancient, rusted screens on the side facing the creek. About half an hour later, I saw a short, scrawny man wearing a baseball cap walk up the hill from the creek, carrying a plastic tub. He ducked into the shack, the screen door slapping shut behind him.

I climbed out of my truck, walked toward the shack, and poked my head in through the open screen door. Water was running into the big metal sinks where he was hunched over shucking the first of his catch.

I knocked on the door frame. "Excuse me. Are you Jeff Mc . . . ?"

My tongue went numb as he turned from the sink holding a shucking knife in his right hand. His long, dishwater-blond hair was pulled back behind his head. He glared at me with piercing tan eyes. The color of creamed coffee.

Carol's words crackled in my head like I was tuned to a tiny, tin-sounding AM receiver in my ear. . . . *The one that stayed behind killed him . . . He's a blond . . . dirty blond . . . Bad teeth . . . those eyes. They are so unusual.*

This was him. This was the guy. I was looking right into the face of the man Carol had described as Frank's killer. He looked like he hadn't bathed in days.

"That's right," he said roughly, a cigarette dangling from his mouth. "What do you want?"

"I . . . I'm . . ." I stammered, trying to regain composure. "I'm in town working on a story and thought you might be able to help me out."

"What kind of story?" he said with half interest.

"Well, it's about that guy they found murdered in the woods across the road back in '82," I said.

"The boy in the woods." He nodded matter-of-factly. "I don't know nothin' about that." He shrugged and turned back to his work in the sink. He shouted over his shoulder above the gurgle of slow running water. "I done talked to the police about that already. I told 'em all I know."

"Well, maybe you could tell me about Tommy McDowell," I said, trying to change the subject. "I understand he was a suspect. Do you think he could have done something like that?"

Jeff slowly turned around and removed the cigarette from his mouth. He flashed a creepy smile, revealing a mouth full of nasty, gnarled, smoke-stained teeth. "Tommy McDowell." He nearly spit the words.

A rushing fever-hiss returned to my head and blood pumped . . . *pockita, pockita* . . . like an old steam engine against my temples. The only thing going through my mind was, *Tattoo, tattoo*, as I kept looking at his right wrist to see if I could catch a glimpse of faded blue ink. The sight of a tattoo would make Carol's vision complete. Unfortunately, he wore a long-sleeved shirt, and his hands were covered with wet muck.

"Tommy McDowell was a coldhearted son-of-a-bitch," Jeff drawled. "So, yeah, I s'pose he coulda done somethin' like that. I don't know; I didn't know him that well."

"But didn't you grow up around here and hang out with some of the kids in town?"

Jeff now seemed to be making every effort to maintain continuous, undiverted eye contact with me, as if trying to convince me he was telling the truth by looking at me straight-on. "Yup. But I was a few years younger than Tommy. I didn't hang around him much. He was . . . creepy . . . if you know what I mean."

Yeah. Creepy. His beady, caramel-colored eyes were making me nervous. I tried to break his stare. "Did you ever play in those woods back there?"

"Sure, but like I said, I didn't hang out much with them kids." He slowly turned the shucking knife over and over again in his hand.

"Well, tell me a little bit about Murrells Inlet. I understand it was a pretty wild place back then."

"Yup. We been known to raise a li'l hell 'round here." He chuckled, taking a drag of his cigarette. Then he looked back at me, sort of sizing me up from toe to head, and slowly exhaled smoke in my direction. "But I imagine our idea of raisin' hell's a li'l bit differ'nt 'n yers."

"I . . . suppose you're right." I was trying not to let my face show that my bowels were on the verge of releasing their contents right there on the concrete floor.

With a dismissive turn, Jeff went back to shucking his oysters. He grumbled over his shoulder. "I'll prob'ly only make a measly twelve bucks for my catch today. That means I only need to make another four thousand, nine hundred eighty-eight dollars to pay off my land."

I started backpedaling toward the screen door, pushed it open with my back, and let it slap shut with a piercing thwack. "Hey, look. I've bothered you enough," I hollered through the screen. "Thanks for your time."

Jeff turned and skittered to the door. He held it open and called after me with a condescending head cock, "Good luck on yur story."

I didn't know I could walk backward that quickly. "And, uh, good luck paying off your land," I said, bumping into my truck.

"And, hey," he said with a squint, "I'd watch it if I were you. This town talks."

I hopped in, fumbled with my keys, and started the truck. As I pulled out of the shell-strewn drive, I glanced in my rearview mirror and caught a glimpse of Jeff McKenzie standing with the screen door propped open, looking after me. He had a kind of *holy shit* look on his face. I'm sure some plucky, would-be-private-eye driving up with out-of-state plates and asking questions about a murder must have put a flutter in his gizzard.

I gunned my truck and whipped it back onto Business 17, throwing sand across the pavement, and headed for Georgetown. It was close to five o'clock, and I wanted to catch Detective Medlin before he left the sheriff's office for the day.

I tried to release some of my adrenaline by talking out loud to myself and pounding on the dashboard. "That was him. It had to be him. I can't believe it. Man, Medlin is going to freak when I tell him." But suddenly I had second thoughts. "Maybe I shouldn't tell him. He'll think I'm crazy. No, of course, I have to tell him. This is important."

For the next twenty minutes I fidgeted in my seat, talking myself into and out of telling Medlin. By the time I pulled into the driveway of the bed-and-breakfast, it was already past five, and I was hell-bent on telling somebody. I went in through the kitchen door and straight to the refrigerator. I retrieved a bottle of beer, popped the top, and started pacing — sipping and practicing out loud what I would say to Medlin. And at this point, I'd have to call him at home. Finally satisfied with my spiel, I grabbed the portable phone and punched in his number.

"Hello, Bob? This is Jim."

"Well, hello, sir." All week he had addressed me as "sir."

"Hey, look," I said, "I know it's after office hours, but I need to tell you about some stuff that's happened over the past couple of days. You got a minute?"

"Sure."

"Take it any way you'd like, but just please hear me out."

"I understand," he said patiently. "Take your time."

"So, for what it's worth . . ." I launched into the whole story about Carol going to the scene of Frank's murder, about the description she gave, about the boom box, about seeing a shrimp boat with a similar name, and about how I had just stood face-to-face with the man she had described. With each bit of info my voice pitched higher and higher.

"Okay, okay," he said. "Just take it easy."

"You probably think this is crazy."

"No, I've heard crazier," he said. "Tell me, what was the make of the boom box?"

"It was a Radio Shack brand."

"And you say the brother's Social Security number is engraved on the back?"

"That's right. He gave me the number this morning if you want it," I said excitedly. "Is there any possibility of recovering it?"

Medlin spoke in the measured cadence of a seasoned lawman. "Well, it would be pretty difficult to get a search warrant on this kind of information. And besides, we've already questioned the fella you met, and everyone else in town, and came up with nothing.

We'd have to have pretty strong evidence to go back in and stir things up."

"Right," I said, "I guess this kind of stuff wouldn't be admissible in court."

"That is correct."

"Have you ever worked with a psychic?" I asked Medlin.

"No, but I've heard of people using them for this sort of thing."

"Do you believe in that sort of thing?"

"No," he said quickly, but then he paused. "Well, I don't know if I do or if I don't. Some of the stuff they say is pretty coincidental. But let me tell you something, there are a lot of times in this business when we know something has happened, but we can't say it happened. I mean, things that we know — in our hearts — to be true. And when you can't prove it in a court of law, it's frustrating. But unfortunately, what you have to do is turn your back and walk away." As a not-so-subtle warning, he added, "And, Jim, I suggest you do just that."

EARLIER THAT DAY, Carol had checked out of the bed-and-breakfast and returned to North Carolina. I called her at home that night.

"Hey, Carol, I'm convinced this guy I met was the one who killed Frank. The one you described with the tan eyes and messed-up teeth."

"It sounds like it. Were you scared?"

"Well, yeah, sort of. But what could he have done in broad daylight?" I said. "Although he was holding a shucking knife. I guess he could have slit me open like an oyster."

Carol didn't laugh.

"Anyway," I continued, "you said you saw three men standing there in the woods. Right?"

"Right," Carol said.

"And you said that the one who pulled the trigger was the shortest of the three. Well, this guy I met today was not much taller than me. I'm about five-foot-seven, Tommy was about six feet tall, and

Frank, he was somewhere in between, about five-nine or five-ten. Is that about how you saw it?"

"Yes, it was. Go on," she said.

"Well, my guess is that Tommy's the one who left to get the pot. And I bet he was going to get it from Paul Nance, the one who owned the restaurant. Everyone in town knows he used to run drugs, which would explain why the tall guy insisted on going alone. Maybe Paul didn't want anyone else to know he was involved in drugs. And one of former employees told me that shortly after they found Frank's body, there was a rumor that Paul had him killed because of something drug-related. And remember that shrimp boat you saw? The bookkeeper at the restaurant told me it was Paul's boat, and the family has been trying to sell it since he died."

"No kidding?" she said. "And when I had the vision of that boat, it wasn't in the water. That's wild."

"And you said they drove north in two cars. Well, I was thinking that they could have taken Frank's car and that dark, junky Buick you saw. You know, so that they could ditch Frank's and take the other one back. It wouldn't have taken them but a couple of hours to drive up there and back. Wilmington's just over the state line."

"Yeah. But why would they drive it all the way into Wilmington? They could have just left it in some woods right on the other side of the border," Carol said.

"I don't know, maybe they weren't smart enough to think about that. Anyway," I continued excitedly. "Then you mentioned that you heard one of them saying, 'You have to be Frank.'"

"Right," she said.

"Well, I was thinking that he was probably saying something like, 'You've got to pose as Frank.' You know, like, 'Take his license and drive his car until we can dump it.' One of them had to drive it," I said.

"Sounds possible."

I was getting excited now trying to solve the whole thing. The theories and explanations seemed to pop in my head as fast as I was saying them.

"And all that stuff about Tommy being the one who did it and breaking down in tears in that cop's car, well, maybe he was just so upset about what happened that he couldn't bear it. I think he was probably involved, but he probably only intended on rolling Frank for some money or whatever. I don't think he ever intended to kill him, but when he got back and saw what his buddy with the bad teeth had done, he sort of freaked. You know he'd never been busted for any violent crimes. It was always little bullshit stuff like forging checks and using other people's credit cards. I don't think he had the balls enough to shoot anybody." I paused. "I'm sorry, I'm rambling."

"No, no. It's all right. It sounds like you could be right."

"And then a couple of days go by and Tommy feels like shit about the whole thing, so he calls the cops and says he just found the body. It makes perfect sense to me."

"Me, too," she agreed.

"And maybe Paul Nance helped them cover up the whole thing so his name wouldn't be associated with it. Which would explain why he told his sister on his deathbed that Tommy didn't do it. But he obviously wasn't willing to say who did."

"The whole thing is pretty wild," Carol said. "But you know what really bothers me is how upset Frank seemed about that argument he had. He had such a strong desire to go home, such a strong bond to home . . ." Her voice trailed off.

"You know, I forgot to tell you, but Frank had argued with his mother the day he left home. And you said that he was thinking about his mother, so maybe that was the argument he was upset about."

"I don't know, but I get the sense that someone in the family was terribly concerned about him, and I'm pretty sure it was his mother." She paused. "Well, have you told the police all of this?"

The question brought me back to reality for a second.

"I told the detective about the boom box and about meeting Jeff McKenzie," I said.

"What did he say?"

"He said there wasn't a whole lot he could do but that he'd talk it over with the sheriff and see what he thought."

"You know, Jim," she said, "there really isn't much they can do. I knew that. I probably should have told you."

"Well, I guess I'd hoped that maybe something would break through. It's been one hell of a wild week."

"Honey, I'm sensing that it's not too safe for you there. I think it's best for you to leave as soon as you can."

By then I'd come to trust Carol. If she sensed something, it was probably true. So, after I hung up, I started packing my clothes and gathering the files and notepads I had strewn throughout the room. Aside from the rustling paper, I could hear the ticking of the antique grandfather clock in the hallway outside my room. The melancholy rhythm heralded the knell of my departure. I felt a bit defeated.

I wasn't any closer to answers. My time in Murrells Inlet had only stuffed me full of questions and sent me slouching toward oblivion. I had come so close, I thought. To what, I wasn't sure. But I knew I was close to something. Only to be stalled like a windup toy that loses its momentum midstride. There I stood, suspended with my eyes wide and hand outstretched.

Similarly, Murrells Inlet had snuffed out the torch Frank McGonigle carried, and he was furious when he realized he was dead. For what had he been denied the opportunity to "find himself" and assume his rightful place in the world? For money? He would have gladly given the guys his money if that's all they wanted. The money didn't mean a damn thing to him.

I tried to sleep that night, anticipating a long drive the following day. But, for a second night in a row, I could only snatch an occasional elusive shred. Several times I'd finally relaxed to the point of breaking over to the other side; I was on the edge — my body completely relaxed, my brain a mush of lava-lamp bubbles and . . . so close . . . when I would be jolted back down to the reality of my mattress and my sweaty-necked pillow. I surrendered shortly before dawn, not to sleep, but to the demons that tugged at my ankles. I quietly rose and washed my face in the basin in my room. I ran some water through my matted hair and dressed in the predawn chill.

chapter eighteen

I slipped out of town that morning just as the sun released its first cotton-candy rays out of the Atlantic. I drove over the bridge spanning the Waccamaw River and slowed down to soak in my last view of the glistening pink-morning sea. A gaggle of gulls dove and swooped and hovered over a lone shrimp boat that chugged resolutely back into the bay. The masts of its net cranes looked like arms stiffly waving farewell as the boat bobbed from side to side.

As I sped up through the interior of South Carolina, on the first leg of my twelve-hundred-mile trek back to Kansas City, Carol was back home in North Carolina, running some of Frank's information through the astrological software on her computer. By early afternoon I felt like I was far enough away from the coast to relax a little and stop looking in my rearview mirror. I began to feel the effects of two sleepless nights, so I decided to check into a motel near the outlet malls in Sevierville, Tennessee. As soon as I keyed my way into the room, I called Carol to see how things were going.

"I tried to pinpoint the exact date and time of Frank's death," she said. "Now, going on information from the coroner's and sheriff's reports, I estimated the date to be Saturday, the twelfth of June 1982. And I figure it had to have been in the afternoon, because while we were in the woods the other day, I heard distant thunder. And you told me that the paper had said that there were some heavy thunderstorms that afternoon. Right?"

"Yeah, that's right." I kicked off my shoes and stretched out on the plywood-firm bed.

"And then, this time kept poppin' into my head — three thirty-eight, three thirty-eight. So, I just entered those numbers into my computer along with the longitude and latitude of Murrells Inlet."

"What happened?"

"Well, my computer then kicked out the alignment of all the stars and planets at that precise moment," she said, as if that were supposed to mean something to me. "Darlin', I think we hit it right on the head."

"Hit what on the head?"

"Frank's death was karmic," she said, starting to get excited. "That boy was supposed to die that day. There was no way around it. It was his day."

"What do you mean?" I asked. "How do you know?" By that time, I should have known better than to ask Carol how she knew.

"Just by looking at the way these planets are aligned," she said. "At first I didn't see this boy's sun rise. And the sun always rises. He was destined to die."

"Anything else?" I asked. "You got anything else on that day."

"Yes," she continued softly. "He was feeling good that day. He had an unusual amount of self-confidence. He felt like he had made some friends, but there was deceit, much deceit. The ones he had placed his trust in deceived him."

"He must have been feeling confident if he asked that guy if he could tag along with him to get the pot. That's something he would never have done," I said. "He was probably on a real high, since he'd just gotten away from home and met some new friends . . ."

"But then they deceived him," Carol added.

"You mean, they killed him."

She sighed. "That's right."

"Hey, Carol, I just thought of something." I sat up in bed. "You remember I told you about that big storm that hit the day Frank left home. Could you enter the coordinates for Kansas City and see what was going on with him that day?"

"I sure could," she said. "You got the day and date?"

"Yeah." I clamped the phone receiver between my ear and my shoulder as I rose from the bed. "I've got all my files right here. I photocopied the front page of *The Kansas City Times* from the day he left home, and I copied all the stories about the storm. Hang on a second while I fish it out."

I dropped the receiver and grabbed my plastic file box from where I'd left it near the door. I set it on the bed, flipped open the lid, and dumped the contents out over the polyester bedspread. I shuffled through the folders and loose sheets and snatched out my news-clip file.

"Okay, here it is," I said, reading as I spoke. "The date was Monday, June 7, 1982. The storm hit the city before dawn, but they think Frank left sometime in the afternoon, between noon and two o'clock."

"So, why don't we say that he left at one o'clock, just to get an idea of what was going on." I could hear her pecking away at her keyboard as she spoke. "I should have some output here in just a minute."

I flipped to the next page, which was a copy of the continuation of the news story on the storm, when I noticed a separate three-sentence item at the bottom of the page.

"Hey, Carol. Wait a second. Listen to this . . . 'Solar flare recorded at center in Colorado. The largest solar flare since July 1978 was recorded Sunday at the National Oceanic and Atmospheric Administration center, a spokesman said. The flare at ten thirty-seven A.M. was so large that it went off the center's scale and was gauged through manual calculations. Forecasters expect the flare to cause magnetic disturbances and disruption of short-wave radio communications today.' Would that have any effect on Frank's chart for that day?"

"You bet it would, honey. Solar flares are notorious for affecting the moods and the mental synapses of animals. It has the same effect that full moons have on people." Her computer printer beeped and whirred in the background. "Oh, my Lord, honey, lookie what we have here . . ."

"What've you got?"

"You won't believe this, Jim, but the moon was full the night before he left home. The place was up for grabs!" Carol nearly shouted. "Frank's brain was reeling. I bet if you checked hospital emergency room records for that day, they'd be outta control."

"But why would it affect him so much?"

"Because he was a highly sensitive person and susceptible to that kind of stuff," she said. "All of the excess energy in the universe that day provided him a burst of energy and self-confidence that helped him decide to leave home. It was that day, or never."

"You mean that some fluke burst of flame on the sun can have that much effect on a person?"

"You bet, honey." Carol sounded almost giddy. "We're talking energy equivalent to a nuclear explosion of hundreds of thousands, perhaps millions, of megatons. When that comes hurtling through space toward earth, it's bound to have some wild effects. Now, I'm not saying it caused Frank to leave home, but that, coupled with the fact that there was a full moon — I think it probably provided the cosmic nudge he needed."

"Carol, is it possible that the storm that blew through Kansas City that morning was the same storm that hit South Carolina later that week?"

"I doubt it. I mean, I'm no meteorologist, but I suppose the two storms possibly could have spun out of the same weather system. I guess five days is really not that long." She paused. "But Jim, I don't mean to sound trite or anything, but I think the real storm was inside that boy. I mean, I get the feeling that Frank was ready . . . he was ready to get outta that place. Like, if he didn't blow outta there, somethin' was gonna blow inside of him. Like he was about to snap. And I was just thinkin', if you're gonna do his story right, you gotta get more info on him."

"Like what?"

"Like more background on his family and his childhood. And didn't you say he was seeing a shrink?"

"That's right."

"Then you got to find out some info about what the shrink had to say."

"I've already interviewed his therapist."

"Then take a look at the notes again. You're missin' something . . .

somethin' about his family maybe . . . I'm not sure, but you'll know it when you see it. Remember, if you want to get a good profile of a person, look at his family. Our families help mold us. I'm just sayin' that it might help you out as you write this thing. Don't take anything for granted."

"All right. I'll start diggin'. And, Carol, thanks for everything. I'll be in touch."

"Okay, honey. You take care, now. Love ya."

"Thanks. Love you, too . . ." Then I shouted into the phone, "Hey, Carol, hang on a second."

"Yes," she whispered. "I'm still here."

"There really are angels, aren't there?"

"Of course," she said with a chuckle. "Honey, what made you think of that?"

"Well, remember when I first met you? You were telling me that you saw those two little boys in the arms of an angel that was standing in your hallway."

"Yes," she said, sounding a little perplexed.

"Well, at the time, I just thought you were a little weird and it was just some sort of vision or something. But since then, everything you have told me has turned out to be true. The shrimp boat. The guy with bad teeth. The boom box. All of it has been right on. So, I was just thinking that if you saw an angel holding those kids, then there must really be angels."

Carol spoke softly. "There sure are, honey. And don't just take my word for it. You can see 'em if you just pay attention. They're here all the time. Just be alert. You'll hear them. And if you get real still, sometimes you can see 'em."

"Thanks, Carol. That's all I wanted to know. We'll talk soon." I hung up.

I COLLAPSED BACK onto the bed, right on top of all my files and papers. On top of all the notebooks full of interviews with the cast of oddball characters who inhabit Murrells Inlet. On top of all the little microcassette tapes encoded with the voices of Frank's family and friends. The papers crinkled and snapped as I rolled over on my back. The muscles in my legs and back twitched ever so slightly. Kind of like my body was slowly letting go of its grip on a taut rope of stress one . . . slow . . . inch . . . at . . . a . . . time. My muscle fibers flitted like the tinkling of little keys on a player piano that magically drop and pop back up all by themselves. I had always loved that sensation, because it meant that a deep, drool-on-the-pillow sleep-fest was seconds away.

I had a dream that afternoon. Possibly the most profound dream I had ever had. I was at a party in a big house, like a fraternity house or something. Lots of noise. Lots of smoke. Lots of warm bodies talking loudly and drinking heavily. I stood talking with a group of close friends I did not recognize. Suddenly someone pushed his way through the crowd and entered our little circle of discussion. It was Jeff McKenzie.

By now, he had come to represent everything I feared in the world . . . ignorance, violence, filthiness, and downright nastiness. His demonic tan eyes locked on me. His snaggle-toothed grin dripped saliva. He walked right up to me, put his nasty, stinking face in mine, and poked my chest with his crusty-nailed index finger. He said, "Hey you little college prick. You'd better watch yourself. The next time I see you, I'm gonna kick your ass." Then he turned and disappeared back into the crowd.

I was frantic. My friends told me not to worry, but I had a nauseous feeling that I wasn't going to avoid the wrath of Jeff McKenzie.

I turned from my unfamiliar old friends and ran up the huge staircase of the house. Suddenly I was overwhelmed with the sense that Jeff was scared of me. Scared as much as I was of him. I started to feel sorry for him. So, I sat down and wrote him a letter. I told him how I knew he was frightened. I empathized with his state and told him I was pulling for him and would be willing to talk with him anytime he needed me. Then I mailed the letter.

The next scene in my dream must have been later the same night. I slowly descended the stairs of that same massive house; through the spindles of the banister, I saw Jeff across the room. He spotted me, like a father catching a pajama-clad child peering down on his parents' cocktail party. He strode purposefully toward me as I continued down the steps with the stoic face of a convict on his way to the gallows. I flinched when he reached me as he extended his hand in greeting. I stood there baffled as he said, "Hey, Jim, I got your letter. Thanks. I really appreciated it. It was very thoughtful of you. And, you know that stuff I said earlier about wantin' to kick your ass? Forget about it. Hey, I'll see you around." He turned and walked back into the crowd, smiling.

I woke up sopped in drool and sweat. Still, staring up at the ceiling, I listened to the sound of the cars whizzing by outside on the road to Dollywood and felt a sudden urge to get up and write letters to all my fears. But I realized I'd already done it by writing to Jeff McKenzie. He, after all, was my worst nightmare.

I spent what was left of my evening eating a carry-out grilled chicken breast and salad from the steak house next door. I washed it down with a quart of Miller High Life that I bought at the convenience store across the road as I pored over the reams of information I had collected on Frank McGonigle's life. But my mind kept wandering — pondering the wonder of Carol Williams.

I had finally reached a point where I harbored little doubt about Carol's gift or her account of what happened to Frank or her claim that she worked with the FBI. She'd made me a believer, just like she'd predicted. But the journalist in me had to verify something about her. It took me a decade or so, but eventually I called FBI headquarters in Washington, DC, to see if they would admit to using psychics. I spoke to someone in their press office who said he could not comment on the subject but suggested that I contact the Society of Former Special Agents of the FBI (SFSAFBI), as they would be more at liberty to discuss such matters.

Nancy Savage, executive director of SFSAFBI, told me that as a special agent she would take a statement from anyone who had information about a case, regardless of what they called themselves or what powers they claimed to have. "It was important to document all information that was being relayed to [us]. I can tell you the FBI does not work with psychics — as in believing in psychic power."

Then I remembered that a longtime friend of my wife's family, Susan Nitsche, was a retired FBI special agent. I called her, too.

"It doesn't pass my smell test," Susan said. "In my twenty-five years as an agent, I never heard of a case involving a psychic. Not to say that there haven't been cases. The information we gathered had to be fact-based, and we had to confirm the reliability of our sources. A psychic wouldn't be considered reliable."

They clearly hadn't met anyone like Carol.

THE NEXT MORNING before I checked out of the hotel, I called Frank's brother Jerry. I told him all about Carol and her vision in the woods.

"That son-of-a-bitch," Jerry seethed through tears. "He laughed when he shot Frank. I'd like to go down there and beat the shit out of him."

I asked Jerry if he wanted to tell his parents about Carol or if I should. He discussed it with his brother Mike, and they decided that the best way to break the news was for me to tell the family the same way I told them — straight and from the top.

I had about eleven hours of drive time to practice what I was going to say. By the time I had crossed the Mississippi River and was in the home stretch toward Kansas City, I had built up much trepidation about facing the McGonigles. I was concerned that what I had learned from Carol would somehow upset the family, dredging up old feelings and perhaps tearing open old wounds that had begun to heal. I was concerned that the circumstances through which I had learned the information would be a bit too "new age" for people with strong ties to the Catholic faith. But whatever their reaction, I thought, I needed to tell them everything as it happened.

When I arrived back in Kansas City, I arranged a meeting with the McGonigles the next evening. We gathered in the living room of Bill and Joan's townhome in South Kansas City. Billy arrived late, joining his parents and his siblings, Mark, Mike, Joanie, and her husband, Roy. With all eyes and ears set in my direction, I slowly relayed the story, trying not to leave out details.

When I got to the part about meeting Carol, I prefaced my remarks by saying, "She told me a lot of things about the case and about your family that were right on. Now, I don't know what to make of all the information, except for the fact that it is very coincidental. I'll leave it up to you to decide what to make of it."

I handed everyone a copy of a transcription of the tape of Carol's comments in the woods. I played it on a microcassette recorder and held it close to Joan, so she could hear. The others huddled in close to their mother to listen.

As they read along with the tape, Joan frequently shook her head and said, "Oh, dear." And when it came to the part where Carol talked about the short, dirty man with bad teeth laughing about shooting Frank, tears began to flow.

Then Billy muttered from the couch, "You know, I could really look like Frank if I dyed my hair black. I'd like to go down and hang around this guy and just sort of freak him out."

"Yeah, right," Mike said, shaking his head, "like he's going to remember what Frank looked like after thirteen years."

"Hey, once you kill somebody, you never forget their face," said Billy.

"How do you know?"

"That's just what I've heard."

Meeting with the McGonigles that night was heart wrenching and overwhelming. My own mixed emotions overflowed — sorrow, empathy, intrusion, guilt — yet I found the experience fulfilling and felt honored to be the messenger.

"Look . . . I . . . I feel really torn about bringing you this information. Like it's not my place to interfere with your grieving," I told them.

"Nope. You're part of this story, now," said Bill in a matter-of-fact baritone. "You're emotionally tied to this and to all of us, now."

Joan took my hand. "Jim, you know, this doesn't change anything. Frank is still dead, and there is nothing that will bring him back. But I'm so grateful for you and for all you've done to bring us this information. I really want to believe that what Carol said is true. And it's exactly how I've always imagined it happened. It's comforting in its own way. It helps bring a bit more closure to the whole thing for me. I really feel like the Lord had a hand in all of this. Thank you."

Mike agreed. "Absolutely."

"Now, I know some of these kids feel like we should do something about this man who may be responsible for killing Frank," Joan said thoughtfully. "But that kind of reaction would be too laconic for his crime. He's going to suffer. He'll answer to God."

I had learned to love Joan, if just for the fact that she'd use a word like *laconic* in this situation.

THE MCGONIGLES SETTLED into a new sort of peace with the latest developments in their thirteen-year journey to come to an understanding of Frank's life and death. Carol Williams's insight into the thoughts and feelings of a man she did not know provided a comforting closure to the suffering of a family she did not know. Still, Joan and Bill sensed the final words of their saga could not be written until they all were joined together in the next life with their dead son. They were patiently resigned to that heavenly meeting, and I trust they've had their reunion. But they also knew that much could be done while they were alive to heal the wounds of Frank's loss and address any feelings of having been wronged that existed within their family.

They were not ashamed about the past. There were no feelings of humiliation in facing the troubles inherent to families, especially a large, spirited family like theirs. They seemed to have settled into a humble acceptance of wrongs committed, and feelings avoided, and to have taken up a sincere dedication to working toward a better understanding of one another.

"The shame," said Frank's brother Mark, "would be if we turned our backs on the lessons and refused to learn anything from Frank's life."

But even with this newfound peace within the family, there lingered strong feelings that something should have been done to bring Frank's true killer to justice. Several of Frank's siblings expressed frustration in the fact that Frank's murderer might still be wandering free somewhere and might be capable of killing again.

"What pisses me off," Katie said, "is that if this guy did it, he'll get away with it and feel like he's above the law. He may kill someone else. My sense of balance would be greatly enhanced if I knew that the police were pushing a little more to try to convict him."

Katie recalled how Frank was obsessed with fairness. He was adamant about equality in all dealings, whether it was dividing up sandwiches or pouring out glasses of soda — he had to make sure everything was even.

"I don't know if he'd go in for revenge, but he had an awful temper," Katie said. "I've wondered if maybe he had something to do with bringing all of this to light."

In her own twisted sense of revenge, Katie, half jokingly, said she wanted to start sending pictures of Frank from all over the country to this man in South Carolina, just to freak him out. But she knew that would only be petty retaliation, so she tried to intellectualize the experience.

"If there is any lesson that comes out of this, it's that if you hang around people like that, this is what happens. I know there are some who say that people who sell marijuana are not violent. Bullshit! To obtain illegal substances, you have to hang around some pretty scuzzy people."

Mark said that for the few nights following our meeting, while he was up late working on some reports, the images of Frank's murder kept eating at him. Around midnight one night, he went as far as to call directory assistance in South Carolina and track down the number of "that guy." He held on to the number for a few days before working up the nerve to call it. When he finally did call it, the phone rang endlessly. No one answered.

Mark had visions of whispering in the phone, *I know all about the boy in the woods*. But he decided he'd rather just sit and listen to the man's voice if he answered.

Mark's wife, Peggy, had perhaps the most positive suggestion about how to send a message to those in Murrells Inlet who might have been involved in Frank's murder and involved in the cover-up.

"I'd like to see all the members of the McGonigle family — Joan and Bill, the eight remaining siblings, their spouses, the twenty-five grandchildren, aunts, uncles, all descend on Murrells Inlet for a family reunion," she said. "Then everyone could visit the spot where Frank was buried, stop in at Nance's restaurant, and talk to the local press about what happened. Basically, to impress upon the community that someone we loved has been wrongfully taken from us. The emotional impact alone would be enough to cause anyone remotely connected with the murder to squirm in their skin."

Mark agreed with his wife that such a message might have satisfied their sense of justice. Although he's not one for vengeance, he felt compelled to impress upon those responsible that Frank was a real person who was important to him.

"We need to let this guy know," said Mark with determination and a slight quiver of pent-up emotion, "that the rock he threw into our pond has caused many ripples."

PART THREE

roll away
the dew

chapter nineteen

On a crisp autumn evening in 2018, I found myself recounting Frank's story to a rapt audience of extended family and friends on my brother's back patio. My nieces were entertaining some of their college friends. "Uncle Jim, you have to tell them your story about Frank. Please!"

All I needed was an audience. I couldn't resist. I lapped up the bait and leaned forward in my chair, lowered my voice, and began where I always do. "Frank McGonigle left his Brookside home in 1982. His family never heard from again."

Like a seasoned Shakespearean actor performing *Hamlet* for the 112th time, I had the audience in the palm of my hand, pausing at just the right moments for oos and ahs and laughter and gasps. And like many great actors, I artfully hid the dark secret of my wilted self-confidence behind the boldness of my character. Nonetheless, the applause arrived on cue, followed by my curtain call. And as had happened many times in recent years, I was left feeling like an imposter — a charlatan fleecing the audience of their good graces in exchange for the false impression that they were getting a sneak peek into a work in progress.

There was no progress. Hadn't been for twenty-some years.

When I finished that night, my niece hugged me. "You really need to finish writing that story and get it out there."

If only I had a dollar for every time I heard that. But for whatever reason, her words of encouragement that night sparked something I hadn't felt in years — excitement and resolution. I knew it was either hop back on the horse or keep kicking down the same dusty road of barren dreams.

I credit my niece for the inspiration to dust off my notes — literally. They were in a mold-speckled cardboard filing box in my basement, covered with the pathetic grit of inertia. I lifted the lid to find a dozen or so small yellow legal pads full of notes — scrawled in my hasty reporter chicken scratch, dozens of transcribed interviews printed by obsolete dot-matrix printers on paper that had once been white, photocopied articles, police reports, a rubber-banded bundle of floppy disks, and a handful of microcassettes. My rummaging halted when I found a black-and-white copy of a young child's drawing done by one of Frank's nephews. In the upper left corner was a salutation scrawled in marker, TO: GRANDMA. In the center was a large tree. Beneath it lay Frank, frowning and dead in plentiful high grass. Clouds drifted overhead. A flower grew nearby.

This. This is why I needed to continue pursuing Frank's story.

I felt like an archaeologist digging through an ancient muckheap. Hundreds of hours of research and writing and a gazillion hours of angst were crammed into that sixteen-by-twelve box. If the contents had voices, they would groan and whisper intimacies of the intertwining lives stashed into those folders, laden with sadness, fear, worry, anxiety, and hope for closure. The contents seemed to gaze up at me with the mournful eyes of a cowering horde, wrongfully imprisoned and pleading for emancipation. *Set us free!*

As I lugged the box up the basement stairs to my office, the overwhelming task ahead grew heavier with each ascending step. Excuses and justifications flitted through my mind. I hadn't given up, exactly. Life just happened. Other priorities. I fell into a music career that took me on the road. I wrote and recorded songs and produced albums. I moved a few times. I met, courted, and married my wife. We had two children. I took a corporate job that required my attention and at least forty hours of my time each week. I wrote and published children's books. I lived and slept and ate and mowed the lawn and played cribbage with my buddy Bean and napped in a hammock and drank a few beers — important things that make up a life.

But the story lived with me. It became part of me. It wasn't continuously on my mind but would randomly surface, like the wayward wild hair that grows mysteriously from the top of my left ear. Not always visible, but always there. Not a bother, but so periodically apparent that it needed to be trimmed. This had become my story, too. My family knew it, and the McGonigles knew it long before I did.

"Do the next right thing." That became my motto. One step at a time and all that.

So, I started where all seasoned procrastinators attempt to rekindle their passions. I humbly — with a hint of desperation — summoned the great oracle Google. I thought I'd start easy, with the one character in this story who had seemed most willing to talk and had given me the straightest answers — Chris Nance. He was nearly my age. He was affable and inclined to confess the trespasses of his community while somehow maintaining the pretense of loyalty. And he'd actually be someone enjoyable with whom to reconnect.

I typed in his name and hit ENTER.

My shoulders and my hopes slumped when I read the first entry. "Obituary for Christopher Nance."

He couldn't be dead; he was younger than me. Immediately I hoped it was another, more elderly Chris Nance. But as I scrolled through the next few articles, the details obliterated that hope. In 2012, at age forty-four, Chris had been beaten, stabbed, and burned to death in a drunken fight with two other men, one of whom was Chris's nephew. Another twisted tale of violence in Murrells Inlet.

The judge who sentenced Chris's assailants was quoted in one of the articles. "Unbelievable. To add insult to injury, you burned that poor fella's body. That's about as callous as it gets."

STILL REELING FROM the shocking news of Chris Nance's murder, I turned my sights on Jeff McKenzie. Maybe I could track him down. The last time I saw him was on a follow-up visit to Murrells Inlet in the late 1990s. I had found him raking leaves in a neighbor's yard to earn a few bucks. He seemed kind of out of it — wide-eyed and zombie-like. I approached him cautiously as he worked. "Excuse me, Jeff?"

He looked up at me, although one eye seemed fixed on a distant object over my left shoulder. His whole body drooped, and his face was so flaccid and void of animation that I thought he might drool. "Yeah," he said.

"Sorry to bother you. I met you a couple of years ago. I asked you a few questions about the boy in the woods."

He looked down and feebly stroked the grass in slow motion with his rake. "I don't know nothin' 'bout that."

And that was about the extent of our conversation. I found out later he was recovering from a serious head injury after nearly being killed by a drunk motorist who had collided with Jeff as he rode his bike along the shoulder of a narrow road.

I held on to the slim possibility that he'd turned things around in the intervening twenty years and might be willing to reengage. I pecked out his name on my laptop keyboard with a dangling thread of hope.

No such luck.

Three entries for his obituary topped the list. He died of cancer in 2011 at the age of forty-five. This somehow didn't surprise me. But the following entries caught my attention — multiple paid ads for "people search" services.

"View criminal and court records."

"149 results for persons named Jeffrey McKenzie."

It seemed a bit voyeuristic to peruse the misdeeds of a dead man, but I couldn't resist. I bucked up for a $1.99 trial membership and dove in.

The screen populated with a list of court records that started rather innocuously — run-of-the-mill traffic violations, littering, a noise ordinance infraction, and an unleashed dog. As I continued to scroll, Jeff's sad and turbulent life unraveled before me.

> Drugs/Possession of 28g (1oz) or less of marijuana.
> DUI.
> Obtaining property under false pretenses.
> Simple assault and battery. (I didn't know any assault was
>   considered "simple.")

More obtaining of property under false pretenses.

Cruelty to animals.

Public health rules violation.

Shellfish harvesting violation.

More shellfish harvesting violations.

Public drunkenness.

Disorderly conduct, public.

Solicitation with intent to acquire contraband.

Unsafe equipment (shell fishing).

Criminal operation of watercraft.

Breaking into motor vehicle.

Discharging firearm in dwelling.

Use of vehicle without permission.

Criminal domestic violence.

Assault and battery of a high and aggravated nature. (As opposed, I assumed, to "simple" assault.)

I downloaded the document and saved it. Fourteen pages of traffic, misdemeanor, criminal, and felony violations covering the years 1996 through 2011.

"Jeff was no angel," his sister Sheila told me later during a phone interview. "He was a con and liar, but I don't think he would ever kill anybody. It got to the point where I couldn't have him in my life. He was toxic and crazy — it just about tore me up."

As a child, Jeff was a gifted artist. He liked to draw and carve wood. And he was mechanically inclined, constructing his own creek-worthy boat at age ten.

But trouble started early. When he was seven, he was caught trespassing in a neighbor's home with two other boys. As a teenager, he got busted with some pot and went to jail. His father let him sit there for a day to teach him a lesson.

"He was not stupid," Sheila said, "but came across as stupid because he wasn't educated. But he was gullible and easily lured into stuff."

One of Jeff's former neighbors described him as a hard-working guy who could fix anything. As a kid, he was quiet and desperately wanted to fit in. He was a people pleaser who occasionally would go to extremes to look cool and tough. He would tag along behind Tommy McDowell and Chris Nance and do whatever they told him to do. Since Tommy seemed to derive perverse pleasure from manipulating others, Jeff served as the perfect minion.

"He was a patsy," Carol Williams once told me. "He didn't want to kill Frank, but he needed to do something to feel graduated — like a gang member."

chapter twenty

When Carol's number flashed on my phone's screen, I was sitting in my car in the pickup line outside my daughter's school. A surge of blood thumped in my chest and temples.

Pick up? Or call back when we could talk longer?

I had to answer. It had been nearly twenty-five years. Deep breath. Exhale. I slid my finger across the screen and belted out the heartiest greeting I could muster. "Hello, Carol. How are you?"

"Hey, darlin', I'm great!" Her molasses-sweet Carolina drawl took me back to that misty, tequila-flowing weekend in 1995 when we first met. "I was thrilled to get your letter. When I saw KANSAS CITY on the envelope, I knew it was from you. And it's a good thing it came when it did. I'm getting ready to move in a few days."

"It sure is good to hear your voice."

"Aw, you, too, sweetie. So, tell me 'bout you. You married yet? Got a family?"

"Yup. I'm married. I have two daughters."

"Of course you do. I bet you're a good daddy."

My cheeks flushed as I savored the comfort of her sincerity. "I do my best. So, you know I've decided to revisit the story of Frank McGonigle's murder. You remember Frank?"

"Darlin', how could I forget him? Remember that day in the woods when he shoved me to get my attention? It was playful and all, but he 'bout knocked me down."

I laughed. "I can't believe I forgot about that."

"Oh, I can see it right now. It's not every day I get pushed by a ghost."

"Hey, I'm hoping to reconnect with some of the folks who were involved back then and resurrect this story. It's been simmering a long time."

She let out her trademark raspy chest chuckle. "Yeah, like a couple-few decades. And you know what? I almost didn't go on that trip."

"You never told me that."

"Oh, yeah, when Mary Helen asked me to tag along, I didn't really want to go — I was so busy with my flooring business. You remember Mary Helen."

"Of course."

"The reason I went was because I had a dream about a week earlier that it made me feel good to be there. And I mean more than just staying out all night and getting drunk on margaritas and Grand Marnier. More than that, I was pleased that I went. When I woke up, it wasn't clear what the dream meant, but the feeling was clear. So, I agreed to go."

"I'm glad you did. It changed everything."

"Oh, honey, I was there for a reason. And I hope you know that there are good reasons for the timing of this. You're ready to finish this story now. Back then you didn't have the maturity and insights you do now. And honey, you got a surprise comin'."

"Really? Is that a good surprise . . . or . . . not?"

"Oh, you're gonna be blindsided by something on this — in a good way."

When Carol Williams uses a word like *blindsided*, you pay attention. She knows things. She sees things that others don't. And she's usually right. But remember, don't ever call her a psychic. She doesn't care for that.

"Well, I'm glad to hear it's gonna be good. So, you up for helping me with this?"

"You know if you ask, I have to say yes. That's the way it works. But you should know that I haven't dabbled in this for quite some time. I had to learn to control it to protect myself from the negative energy. In fact, I literally prayed that I wouldn't have those visions anymore."

"Did something bad happen?"

"Nothing like that. It's just that I kept pickin' up energy everywhere I went. At restaurants, at the grocery store. I was in a casino a while back and walked past a guy who was sitting at a slot machine and he was about to get up. I got a strong feeling and told him, 'Don't quit yet. Stay on that machine.' He thought I was crazy. A few minutes later I heard bells going off, and he tracked me down in the bar and bought me a drink to thank me. It just gets overwhelming."

"Well . . . hey, if this is going to be too much for you, I completely understand."

"Don't worry, honey. I'm in."

chapter twenty-one

I've always been sort of a wimp when it comes to confrontation. I'm a lover not a fighter. As the youngest of eight loud and opinionated children, I was often the kid in tears standing in the middle of the chaos, shouting, "Can't we all just get along?"

That may be why my career as a journalist veered quickly toward features and puff pieces. I could talk all day long with people about happy things — their careers, their passions, their dreams. I once wrote about a couple who met each other digging graves and were married in a mausoleum. I flew along with a pilot who used vacation time from her bookkeeping job to fly harrowing missions in her single-engine plane to deliver medical supplies to remote Mexican villages. I interviewed partygoers on the streets of Moscow at three in the morning. My subjects tended toward the light and fun and fascinating. But if it ever came to poking at skeletons in their closets, I'd dance right around them and fumble-step out the door.

Because of this limp-noodle-ness, I often felt awkward and self-conscious around the McGonigles. They're lovely people and kind and certainly accommodating. I just cared too much about what they thought about me. I didn't want to be too pushy or get too personal. I didn't want to expose too many raw nerves or appear to be a voyeur imposing on their grief. And I didn't want them thinking I had appropriated their story as my own. When weeks of research and interviews turned into months, and my phone calls and in-person interviews turned into marathon sessions, their full-and-eager cooperation slowly turned to tolerance, which eventually gave way to them just humoring me. And when I showed up again in their email threads and voicemail boxes a couple decades later without a finished product, I sensed they were kind of over and done with me. Can't say I blame them. Frank wasn't my brother, and he wasn't my friend. Hell, I didn't even know him. But after twenty-five years, I felt like Frank and I were companions on a road trip or at least some sort of distant cosmic cousins. I was invested in a way that I didn't think any of the McGonigles could fully understand — and I didn't think I could ever adequately explain it to them.

In an attempt to stake a claim to the part of this story that was mine, I felt motivated to plunge back into the deep end. It was more than just a desire to prove something or a whimsical aspiration to indulge my self-esteem — it was an elemental need, like the needs for food, shelter, and belonging. I had to go back to Murrells Inlet, sit down with the remaining players, and ask the questions I had failed to ask. I needed my own sense of closure.

I reached out to the person I usually go to first — after my wife, of course. The one I trust when it comes to matters of creativity and writing and storytelling and the one with the deepest connections to the McGonigles — my brother Tom.

Even though he's my older brother by seven years, he and I share many similarities as the youngest of our subfamilies — he the youngest of the first set of four children and I the youngest of the second set. We're both attention seekers — performers perpetually seeking an eager audience or even a not-so-eager one. We both love chasing down a good story and have been known to act impulsively.

Tom was visiting Kansas City on his annual autumn pilgrimage to the lower forty-eight from his home in Alaska. He was staying for a week in our basement. One night, as we stood together in the kitchen cleaning up the dinner dishes, I announced my plan — not exactly seeking advice, just some brotherly validation. "I've decided to head back to South Carolina and dig into Frank's story again."

"Ha! Fabulous." When Tom thinks you've said something even mildly interesting or humorous, his head tilts back and he lets fly a full-throttled "Ha!" that's fueled by a blast from deep in the lobes of

both lungs. If you're telling him a story, and he's standing, he'll shuffle his feet and swerve his hips in anticipation of the punch line, like
a giddy child waiting in line to see Santa Claus. He's a guy you want
in your audience. He's a guy you want on your side.

"This is great. So, when are you going?"

"Well, I'm not sure yet. Things are kind of hectic right now with
school just starting back up for the girls. Money's tight. My sched-
ule's booked up for the next six months or so."

"Look, Jim, you need to do this. You can always come up with
excuses not to. Unless you commit to it, it's never gonna happen.
That's why you still haven't finished this story."

I just nodded and rinsed off a plate in the sink. I knew he was
right.

"All that stuff you just mentioned can be worked out. Especially
with the help of a good wingman." He flashed a grin and held out
his hands. "And it just so happens that Alaska Airlines flies into
Charleston, and I have the miles to get there for free. Let me help.
It'll be a rush."

Tom had a long history as an adrenaline junkie and was always
looking for the next fix. Also, he excelled as a schmoozer with a gift
for shoehorning his way into situations. I thought I had prepared
myself.

"Yeah . . . well . . . thanks," I said. "But I kind of planned on going
by myself. I just want to look up a few people . . . you know, see if I
can find any new clues."

"That's exactly why you need someone to watch your back."

"I don't know. I was looking forward to some alone time — so I
can write."

"C'mon. I'll stay out of your way. I'll just be there for moral
support. You can't go down there alone."

I exhaled loudly enough for him to hear. "You always want to be
the fly on the wall, don't you? Can't stand being left out."

"Exactly. Do you blame me?" He started pacing the kitchen. He
stroked his gray-flecked auburn beard, which usually meant he was
slipping into a deeper mode of cogitation. "I'll tell you what. I'll rent

the car. I'll drive and handle the logistics — which have never been your strong suit. I'll be your expediter."

Tom has talked me into many things over the years, some against my better judgment. Like the time when I was fourteen and he talked me into stealing a neighbor's cast-iron lawn jockey so he could give it to a buddy of his. That was the only time I ever stole anything. It still haunts me.

Despite that memory, I felt myself starting to soften. I supposed I could use his creative input, and it's always nice to have someone to share an experience. And although I hadn't admitted it up until then, I was a bit nervous about heading back into a town where the locals had been eager to run me out.

"Okay. Fine," I said, trying to sound decisive. "But you've got to let me do it the way I need to do it."

Over the next couple of months, as I continued to write and reach out to my contacts, Tom and I wrangled over details and dates, but committed to make the trip happen.

On one of our many planning calls, I said, "If we're gonna get a breakthrough, we need one of the McGonigles to come with us. But which one? We don't want a whole gang descending on that place."

"There's really only one choice," he said. "It's got to be Mike. And you need to be the one to invite him. It's got to come from you."

I reached out to Mike, and we exchanged texts over a couple of weeks. He was unsure at first — work schedules to consider, old emotions to sift through — but when he eventually came around, all of my misplaced angst was subdued by the excitement that this was actually going to happen. "I've never been down there," he wrote. "Never had the chance until now. I'm in."

Five months later, in April 2019, Mike and I stepped out of the Charleston airport a little past noon on a Tuesday. The feel of warm, moist Lowcountry air settling on my forehead immediately took me back to my previous visits more than twenty years prior. Tom, who was not accustomed to sultry climates, had arrived from Juneau the night before and was waiting at the curb for us in a rental car with the air-conditioning blasting.

"Hey, guys. Welcome." Tom beamed as he hopped out of the car to give us hugs. "I picked up some sandwiches and drinks — they're in the cooler in the back. So, unless you need to stop somewhere, we can hit the road right away."

Our first stop was a reunion I had coordinated with Carol Williams at a state park about an hour west of Charleston. We picked a spot close to I-95 between her home and where we were heading. I felt a bit antsy and preoccupied about seeing her after all those years — nervous, excited, curious — like I was reconnecting with an old girlfriend. And I felt oddly accountable for whether the guys liked her. Would they think she was too out there? Would they consider her a phony? After years of describing her and her involvement in this story, I hoped she would live up to the hype. She did not disappoint.

When Carol stepped out of her car at the state park, she stood tall and bright, like a lean Carolina pine with short, curly graying hair and shining brown eyes. She squeezed me tight and then held me at arm's length and gave me a grandmotherly once-over. "God, it's good to see you."

I felt the same way and my face showed it. "You, too. Hard to believe it's been twenty-five years."

"Oh, God, ages ago. But you're just like I remembered you." She hugged me again. "And who are these handsome fellas?"

I introduced her to Mike and Tom, and we moved into the shade to a picnic table at an open campsite. Tom stood and stretched his legs and back in silence while the rest of us sat at the table. Mike and Carol didn't waste any time before jumping into conversation. I let them do all the talking.

"Mike, the first time I met your brother, he 'bout pushed me down!"

"That's what I heard."

"Oh, it was all in fun. He was just trying to get my attention."

Mike leaned forward and folded his hands on the table. "So, tell me about that night."

"Well, as soon as he got my attention, the whole atmosphere lightened up around us." She looked at me and grabbed my wrist. "Remember that? It got really warm. I could feel the tension and anxiety kind of evaporate into the mist that was there. When he pushed me, I knew then what his touch was like, what his energy was like. I communicated with him without speaking out loud and asked him, *What else is there that you have not finished? I thought you would have gone over.* And he told me he couldn't go over. He couldn't go to the other side. And he wanted to make sure that his mother and his father and his whole family would know how much he thought of them and how proud he was to be part of them — the whole family. And that it was really lonely where he was. I don't know why Frank didn't go home, but he was still there."

"He was connected to that spot, by that trauma," Mike said.

"Exactly. But I told him it was okay now. And I promised him, *Jim is going to take the message home. He knows your brothers, he knows your mother, he knows your father. He's from your hometown, and he's here for the specific purpose of trying to find out what happened to you.* So, I don't know why he stayed around there."

"Well, he did travel. He came to my house one night."

Carol reached across the table and touched Mike's hand. "Oooo, did you see him?"

"No, but I felt him."

Mike proceeded to tell Carol about what led up to his encounter with Frank. It was the spring of 1991 — the year the McGonigles found out what had happened to Frank. Mike and his wife, Jennifer, were taking a class at a local community college about spirituality and religion. There was a section on how various religions view the afterlife. The lecture began with the premise that Christians are raised believing that the God they worship is a trinity — Father, Son, and Holy Spirit. The professor then presented a theory based on the Huna religion of ancient Polynesia, that each person is composed of a trinity. Your low self, your middle self, and your high self. Part of the Huna teaching is that when people die suddenly, their spirits become detached from their bodies. And without the energy generated by their bodies, their spirits can't conceive of new thoughts. These spirits who get separated suddenly are in a place where they can't even realize they're dead, because that would be a new thought, and they don't have the energy to fuel that thought.

His summation was that when people are disembodied, they're just drifting. They're lost sailors in need of some catalyst to realize that they have passed on.

"So, all of this was new and different and fascinating to me. My wife is very in tune with this spiritual stuff, where I'm more of a skeptical, pragmatic kind of guy. But to me it was a scientific explanation of what has been given to the mystics all of these years. At some point in time, the religions said, *Scientists, you've got no business messing with God. You do your science, and we'll take God over here. And you stay away from our God.* It was fascinating to me."

Carol was eager to jump in. "I agree with you. It is scientific. Every time someone says I'm psychic, I say I'm not. I have nothing to do with it. I read energy. I connect with energy. And it is a meshing and a recognition of the energy."

While Mike and his wife were taking the class, the ninth anniversary of Frank's disappearance rolled around. It was the seventh of June. And just like they had on the previous eight anniversaries, Mike's parents arranged to have an evening mass offered at St. Peter's in honor of Frank. Mike had to work, so he didn't make the mass. At least that was his excuse. But he agreed to join his family for dinner after mass.

"My wife and kids went to my parents' house and I came over after work. The moment I walked into the house, I was stricken with the worst headache I think I've ever had. It was like a piercing pain shot right through my head behind my eyes." Mike poked his temple with an index finger. "I lay on the couch for two hours while everybody talked and laughed and reminisced about Frank. I didn't even eat dinner. Finally, I told my wife, 'We've got to go home and get the kids to bed.'"

When Mike lay down that night, he fell immediately asleep. At about three o'clock the next morning, Jennifer shook her husband's arm. "Mike, wake up," she said in an excited whisper. "There's somebody in the house."

Mike reluctantly rolled over. "C'mon, there's no one here."

"No, seriously, I can hear the footsteps. They're just walking around the house. They're pacing."

Mike got up and shuffled into the hall, checked on the kids' rooms, and looked around the living room. Nothing. All clear. As he stopped in the kitchen, he remembered how Frank, in his last months at home, used to wake in the middle of night and pace around for hours. He was an insomniac.

Mike grabbed a glass from the cupboard and leaned over to draw some water from the watercooler. Suddenly the hair on the back of his neck stood on end, and he sensed an overwhelming feeling that somebody was standing right behind him. He straightened himself and, without turning around, said, "Look, I don't know who you are or what you want, but, Frank, if it's you, we're trying to find you. You've been gone for nine years. We have no idea what happened to you and we all miss you and we all love you and we just want you to come back. Please give us a way to find you."

Just as suddenly as the presence had arrived, it vanished. Mike felt the fear and sadness drain down through his feet into the floor, and his head didn't hurt anymore. He switched off the kitchen light and went back to his bedroom, where he slipped in quietly beside his anxious wife.

"Something really weird happened out in the kitchen. I had this feeling that someone was standing right behind me. I think it was Frank. I told him that we were looking for him."

"Mike, you're really freaking me out," Jennifer said as she pulled up the covers and huddled close to her husband. They both just lay there quietly for a while holding each other until they fell asleep again.

When Mike told the instructor of his course about what happened, the teacher said spirits are capable of causing physical pain to people as a means of relaying a message. Perhaps the headache Mike experienced was Frank's way of letting Mike know what happened. Before any information about Frank's death had surfaced, the instructor told Mike, "Maybe Frank is dead and maybe he got hit in the head." Several weeks later, of course, Mike and the rest of the family discovered that Frank had been shot in the head.

Mike kind of shrugged when he retold that story. "I believe in that stuff, but I'm not sure to what extent I believe it. It was just a really weird experience."

Carol nodded and smiled knowingly. "He needed to be told he was dead. He didn't know."

Mike nodded. "Exactly. It was less than a week later that the police detective from KCK called my mother and said, 'I found Frank's file.' And that was the beginning of us finding him. It was two months later he called with a match."

The pitch of Mike's voice began to rise as his eyes dampened. "And he came over and told us the story of the boy they found in the woods with a bullet in his head." He made a chopping motion with his right hand. "Boom!

"And I believe if I hadn't taken that bizarre class and if I hadn't recognized what was happening in the kitchen that night, we may never have found him. My skeptic, pragmatic mind looks at it and says . . ." He shrugged. "But in my heart, I know something is there."

"And you have a good heart. I can feel it." Carol's voice swirled calm like a warm, delicate breeze. "And you're a good father."

"Well, thanks. Sometimes I'm not too sure about that. So, how long have you had this ability to . . . know things about people?"

"I feel like I've been a receiver since I was a child. I can't tell you how many times I was spanked for telling hideous stories. And then they began to realize that the hideous stories were sometimes predictions of what was happening. Sometimes something would happen, and they'd say, 'Oh, my God, Carol talked about that.' Or 'Do you remember when Carol said this would happen?' My cousins used to laugh at me and say, 'Carol sees ghosts.' And I did — all the time. And it freaked me out. I could see them and feel them. They all didn't believe me until we were older."

Carol is one of those people I'm proud to have attracted into my life. I wanted everyone to know the cool stuff she'd done and for them to know we were friends. "You've come a long way from that freaked-out kid. Since then, you've helped solve a bunch of cases, right?"

She beamed. "Oh, yes. I've worked with dozens of police departments on many, many cases and with the FBI three or four times. But it's a lot to take in. I mean, how do you tell somebody that their son is going to die? I've had to learn to let things go. My brain is not big enough to store it all. I worked for years to cut it off all together, but I couldn't.

"I'm a believer that if I pick something up, or I have a dream about you, that if you want to know, I'm obligated to tell you, but if I don't tell you, then it comes back on me. It's like being dishonest — withholding information. If I embellish or add or subtract anything, then there's a punishment for me for not being honest. Sometimes I feel it physically."

At the risk of putting Carol on the spot, I asked, "Would you mind telling us about some of the bigger cases?"

"Well, I told Susan Smith to her face, 'You murdered your children, and I know it.' She started screaming at me and the police had to escort me out."

"She was the one who drowned her children, right?"

"That's right. And then Patsy Ramsey contacted me after JonBenét died."

Tom chimed in from the periphery where he'd been patiently pacing. "Seriously? JonBenét Ramsey?" His forehead crinkled with disbelief.

"Yes, seriously. I told Patsy, 'I'll work with you, and I'll do the charts, and I will give you everything I can give to you, until the FBI calls me. When the FBI calls, I'm out.'"

"Were you afraid of them?" Mike asked.

"No, just cautious. I had worked with them before. But I had a friend who went to jail because the FBI said she knew more than she could have known, so she must be involved. And it took her months to get out of it."

"So, were you able to help Patsy?"

"My friend Robin and I ran charts for each of the family members. We played with those charts for three weeks. It was phenomenal — the energy. I sat there one day and started to cry because I realized Patsy was dying. She had cancer and didn't have a whole lot of time. I knew she'd die not knowing what happened to JonBenét."

"Do you know what happened to her?" I asked.

"I kept saying, 'Santa Claus. Santa Claus happened to JonBenét. Ask the police about Santa Claus.' Shortly after that I got a call from the FBI. They said, 'We understand that you've had communication with Patsy Ramsey.' That's when I got out. They still haven't been able to decide who killed JonBenét. I can still picture her, and I can still hear that little girl's voice."

I had always thought how exciting it would be to know things like Carol does. But at that moment I finally understood the blessing/curse aspect of her gift. "All this must be a heavy burden for you to carry," I said.

"It's scary because I'm never sure where it's going to take me. A lot of times there's heartache and grief. I've got enough of my own grief most days, and when you start taking on that of those around you, it can get absolutely overwhelming. It gets to the point where you can't block out the fear and anxiety from other people. And then I start thinking, maybe I'm crazy. It'll take you a lot of different places. It'll fool with the pragmatic and scientific and what you believe as a normal human being."

"Sure, I get it," Mike said. "How do you manage day to day?"

"Letting go and letting God is one of the hardest things you'll ever do. If you truly trust God, it will bring you peace."

chapter twenty-two

After a round of hugs and promises to stay in touch, we left Carol and hit the road for Murrells Inlet. We were gifted a sunny spring afternoon for a drive along a two-lane state road that meandered through the lush green heart of the Francis Marion National Forest. When men of a certain age spend long stretches sitting in a car, their prostates create pressures that require sometimes sudden attention. Although towns appeared less frequently than our need for bladder relief, we discovered an abundance of rural roadside churches, the grounds of which provided perfect cover. We meant no irreverence. We merely sought comfort and relief. It became sort of a game. And besides, Jesus gave us the go-ahead. "Come to me, all you who are weary and burdened, and I will give you rest" — Matthew 11:28 (NIV).

Occasionally we'd find a wide spot in the road with choices. "Baptist or Methodist?" Tom asked.

Mike laughed. "I'm thinking Methodist. They seem to have better landscaping."

Watching and hearing them banter was like watching a well-timed comedy routine or two evenly matched codgers pitching a game of horseshoes — no competition, just enjoying the flow while complimenting each other's play and laughing at each other's jokes.

The connection between Mike and Tom was different from the practical, inquisitive relationship I had established with the McGonigles. It was more familiar, looser, easier, and it further magnified the intimacy Tom enjoyed with the family — a closeness I had courted for two decades, but never had. Tom knew Frank and had memories about him. I did not. He was Jerry McGonigle's good friend growing up and as an adult had become good friends with Mike, taking ski trips together in Utah. I had none of that.

Rather than jealous, I felt relieved that Tom had asked to tag along and had prompted me to invite Mike — and I hoped that this unlikely fraternal journey would solidify my relationship with Mike. Also, Tom possessed the natural ability to loosen things up, always animating any gathering or undertaking with his encouraging laughter, his prodding, his understanding of nuance. He gets people. He gets their jokes and their innuendo. His wrinkled forehead and wide eyes let you know not only that he's listening but also that he hears you. He brings emotion — full on and, often, impulsively. When he's mad, he's madder than hell and swears and pokes a finger in the air to make a point. He's not afraid to get up in your mug if he's triggered, a dangerous impulse for a short guy. He inherited my dad's hot Irish temper and softhearted empathy. When Tom feels touched by a poignant moment or a kind gesture, tears well in his pale-blue eyes.

Like Tom, Mike is a natural-born storyteller — animated, patient, well measured, and methodical like a college professor with a folksy Missouri twang and the timing of a seasoned stand-up comic. He was born into a family that was blessed with what the Irish call "blarney" — the gift of gab with the deft ability to spin a tale that sounds undeniably real, despite the facts.

I just sat in the backseat, pressed the RECORD button on my phone, and let the two of them talk.

"I always looked up to Frank," Mike said. "I thought he was smarter, more grown-up, all those things. But there was a point where I realized that I was kind of the big brother now. He was struggling."

"Yup," Tom chimed in. "I had a similar role in our family."

Mike continued, "So, that morning when we argued, and I had my final words with him, that was the culmination of a couple of years of frustration and trying to help and trying to be supportive. But you know when you do something over and over again and you get the same result? Isn't that the definition of insanity? That's where I was. And then to have him disappear, I was like, *Oh, shit, what have I done?* And don't get me wrong, it wasn't all shitty. We did some fun stuff together, and I was probably the closest thing he had to a friend in the last couple of years he was around."

Tom chuckled from the driver's seat. "Oh, I have vivid memories of Frank. Some good laughs. But Frank always seemed to be the guy who got caught if we were doing something. It was like he had a cloud over his head, and you don't want to think it, but then what are the odds of him being murdered? Not that it was his fault, but do you ever get the inkling that he purposely put himself in a dangerous situation?"

"Yeah, for a long time I toyed with the idea that he set himself up to be in this situation because he didn't have the nerve to do himself in. I have no reason to believe he knowingly did that. He was just unaware enough of the world around him that I could easily see him subconsciously putting himself in that position."

Tom agreed. "He was naive."

After riding in silence for several minutes, Mike turned his attention to the present. "So, Jim, what's the plan for this week?"

Truth was, I didn't have much of a plan. "I thought we'd just poke around, talk to a few people."

"Hmmm . . . Uh-huh." With just a few hummed monosyllables and a sideways glance, Mike had a not-so-subtle way of hurling confidence-shredding daggers. I'd seen it before — a slight smirk twitching at the corners of his mouth, like he could see right through my facade into the fumbling neophyte that huddled in the corner of my psyche. I wondered if he ever looked at Frank that way.

I grasped at anything resembling a grip on the situation. "And . . . uh . . . well . . . in the spirit of Frank, I thought we'd just kinda . . . wing it. I mean, that's what he'd do, right?"

Mike seemed somewhat convinced. "Hmmm. I suppose so. Wing it."

And that's what we did. For the next three days we bounced from one thing to the other with the increased expectation of a breakthrough or at least a sliver of understanding into who killed Frank.

We stopped in at the Georgetown County Sheriff's Department to reconnect with Joey Howell, the recently retired former deputy who patrolled Murrells Inlet; we chatted up local shop owners and waiters; we called on Loraine McDowell Rowe, Tommy's mother; and we sat with Cynthia Nance, the wife of Paul and mother of Chris.

Throughout those conversations, names of the same characters were bandied about. But one intriguing name kept bubbling to the surface — Snakeman. He worked for Paul Nance for many years at the restaurant and did whatever else Paul asked — driving, delivering, sitting on coolers. Everyone spoke highly of him, almost nostalgically. When I asked why he was called Snakeman, nearly everyone shrugged. It appears to have been a moniker given in his childhood, because his siblings all had nicknames — Napoleon, Bubba, Marchy, Tom Cat. Later, in his advanced years, Snakeman was known for picking oysters several days a week from the pluff mud of the creek during low tide, and he had become a reliable caretaker for many properties in town — raking, mowing, and cleaning up the frequent storm debris. Problem was — no one could tell me how to reach him.

"He just shows up every now and then looking for work," said one local. "And he speaks in such a heavy Gullah accent, and he's so hard of hearing, it would be nearly impossible to talk to him on the phone."

We were told by a well-meaning (if perhaps racially tone deaf) white woman that Snakeman lived off Turntable Road, once known as the Hot Road, a predominantly African American part of town. She said we could just drive out there and ask anyone sitting in their yard about Snakeman. "That's what those people do. They like to sit out in their yards in the afternoon. You'll find somebody who knows him."

Turntable Road begins on the west side of Highway 17, about as far from the tony waterfront properties as you can get and still be in Murrells Inlet. Dense woods line the south side of the road, and on the north, you'll find intermittent clearings with houses and trailers and a few older wood structures set back off the road, hidden by trees drooping with Spanish moss.

We passed a group of four middle-aged men sitting in lawn chairs in front of a tidy one-story brick house. "Should we stop and ask these guys?" Tom asked.

"Nah, let's keep moving," said Mike, who had volunteered to take over the driving duties.

Up ahead we spotted a clump of cars and pickups parked on the shoulder in front of an older wooden house. About twenty people — young and old — stood in the gravel drive and on the lawn.

Mike slowed but didn't stop. "Hmm . . . looks promising."

About a hundred yards ahead, the road ended at a T stop. Mike turned left and swung into the parking lot of the Gordon Chapel AME church. A white rail fence surrounded a small churchyard cemetery.

"Looks like they just had a funeral." I pointed to a green tent covering a few rows of folding chairs that faced a gaping grave.

From the backseat, I could tell Tom was getting hyped up as he fidgeted in his seat. "Let's head back over to the house with all those people. Maybe somebody there can help us."

We drove back east along Turntable Road, passed the house with the gathering, and made a U-turn that put us right behind the last car parked on the shoulder. I leaned up, poking my head between the two front seats. "It's probably best if I go up there alone."

Tom nodded. "And it's a good idea not to lead with the fact that you're looking for Snakeman. People get suspicious when you're looking for someone."

I stepped out of the car, put on a pleasant smile, and walked confidently, but not too quickly, up the road to the gravel driveway where a young man and woman were leaning against a car.

"Afternoon." I nodded.

The young woman smiled. "Hey there. Can we help you?"

"Yes. Please. I'm a writer working on a history of Murrells Inlet and some of the restaurants around here. You familiar with Nance's?"

"Of course. Ever'body knows Nance's."

"I'd really like to talk with someone who's worked there and might have known Paul Nance." As I said those words, I looked up toward the house when I saw a muscular, twenty-something man walking purposely toward me. His brown skin glistened and bulged out of a tight white tank top. His mouth pursed, and his brow pinched up behind his sunglasses. I sucked in some warm air. When he reached me, he thrust out his hand as a radiant smile spread across his face. He eagerly shook my hand. "Welcome. I'm James. How can we help you?"

"Thank you. I'm James, too. I go by Jim. I'm in town working on a story about Nance's restaurant. And I'd like to find some people who worked there."

"Hell, I worked there when I was in high school. Lotta folks around here worked there."

As he spoke, a flurried muttering of voices erupted from the front porch of the house. A hunched white-haired man shuffled down the wood stairs and tottered across the lawn swinging his cane in our direction. "Scat! Scat!"

James waived at him and shouted. "It's okay, Pops." He turned to me and whispered. "That's my grandfather. He just buried his wife today."

The old man kept swatting at the air. "Go on, now. Git."

"I'm so sorry, sir," I stammered. "Sorry for your loss. I didn't mean to intrude. You've been very kind."

James took his grandfather's arm. "It's all good, Pops." Then he lowered his sunglasses and winked at me with a smile. "It's all good. Y'all take care now." I nodded my appreciation and turned back toward the car.

Mike and Tom had heard the shouting, hopped out of the car, and were trotting up the road toward me. "What was all that about?" Tom asked.

"It seems we unwittingly crashed the funeral."

"Oh." We all walked quickly and sheepishly back to the car.

We never did find Snakeman. One in a string of several disappointments. Someday I hope to catch up with him.

On our way back to the rental condo, we stopped in at Murrells Inlet Seafood to pick up some fresh fish fillets to grill for dinner. Mike knows seafood as well as he knows meat. And he knows how to cook it. So, while he tended to the grill, Tom and I sipped beers on the deck, and I floated a new idea. "What do you think about contacting local media about Frank's story and seeing if we can dredge up some new leads?"

"I think it's a great idea," Tom said. "It might jar somebody's memory. And enough time has passed that they might be more willing to come forward."

"Mike, would you have any problem doing a TV interview?"

"Naw. I've had some experience. It seems like every Thanksgiving they send a crew out to the store to talk about turkeys. I'm in."

It was after 11:00 P.M. by the time I composed and sent emails to three local TV news departments and two local newspapers. By seven thirty the next morning I had my first interested response, from a producer at WPDE ABC 15 in Myrtle Beach. "We'd love to do something on this!"

We arranged to meet the reporter and videographer at ten thirty on the Murrells Inlet MarshWalk on the waterfront side of the Claw House restaurant. The glistening ripples on the creek and the moored boats at the marina made for a charming backdrop. the smell of boiled crab wafted in the warm air.

With his thick salt-and-pepper hair, squinting eyes, and square jaw, Mike looked like a determined George Clooney. He stood tall in front of the camera and smoldered with resolve. "I guess I'm just looking for answers. I'd love to be able to piece together this story. I know there is someone out there who knows something that's going to make me sleep better."

The news crew followed us across the road to some woods near where Frank's body was found. As they captured some shots of us poking around in the brush, my phone buzzed. It was a message from a reporter at another local TV station, WBFN News. She dispatched a cameraman who interviewed Mike and me that afternoon and ended up running a nearly six-minute special report on the evening broadcast.

Mike laid his emotions out there for the viewing audience. "For nine years I did not know what happened to my brother. And it went from hopeful — that maybe he'd just gone out to find his fortune in the world, and we'd hear from him someday — to despair as the years passed. We found ourselves with a knowing that something bad had befallen Frank. But not knowing what that was — that was really difficult and painful."

When it was my turn on camera, I felt like I was given a prime opportunity to appeal to those in town who might be ready to talk now that most of the key players were dead. "I'm willing to bet there are some people out there who didn't know that the boy in the woods had a name. And that the boy in the woods had a family . . . I began to realize that a lot of people in town knew about this, but not everybody was telling me exactly what happened. And I think some people were holding back some information."

The reporter for WBFN, Meredith Helline, made a plea at the end of her story. "Cosgrove and Mike believe people who will see this story know something, no matter how small, about Frank's death. They ask you to help give them peace and reach out to the Georgetown County sheriff's office, or you can send me a Facebook message and I'll put you in touch with Cosgrove."

It worked. Later that night I received an anonymous email that corroborated much of what I already believed.

> I grew up in Murrells Inlet. I was a junior or senior in high school when this occurred. I don't have any evidence or anything of that nature. What I do know is what was being said at the time by other kids in the area. There were three people — Tommy McDowell, Chris Nance and Jeff McKenzie. Tommy would have been around 20, the other two 15 or 16. Tommy was one weird guy. He was a homosexual pedafile [*sic*]. He was probably preying on the other two boys. Chris Nance was a mean hearted person who liked to bully people that were weaker. Jeff was an outcasted person who would follow so called friends. The other kids used to say that they killed this guy for fun. Just to see what it was like. Because of the personalities of these boys, it was easy to believe. Tommy died in prison of aids, Chris was stabbed to death by his nephew and roommate, I believe Jeff died of

cancer. This may be only a rumor, but I knew all three and they were certainly more than capable. It also is ironic all three died horrible deaths. Maybe that was the Lord's judgement.

The person who sent the email agreed to talk with me over the phone a couple weeks later.

For winging it, Mike, Tom, and I felt pretty good about the progress of our quest. With just one day left, we all began to affect the swagger and confidence of less hunky versions of Magnum PI. That evening we feasted on more bounty from the sea and savored the adrenaline. Later, as Mike collapsed into his bed and drifted, he thought about the one thing he really wanted out of this trip. And he was about to get it.

chapter twenty-three

The next morning, Cynthia Nance stood in the entryway of her home, puzzlement wrinkling her forehead. I pulled open the storm door. "Sorry to barge in on you like this, Cynthia. Hope we didn't give you a start."

"That's quite all right. Come on in."

Her surprise was understandable. Mike and I had been there just two days earlier when we had a nearly two-hour conversation with her, while Tom waited for us in the car. We all agreed that one less person in the room might be less intimidating. She had been eager to talk that day and quite at ease inviting male strangers into her home. That meeting had been scheduled. This one had not.

"We're heading out of town, back to Charleston to catch our flight. When we drove past your road, we thought, 'Let's pop in and see Cynthia really quick before we go.'"

"Well, good. Have a seat." She waved us toward the living room and smiled as if we were old friends. She moved her short, solid nearly eighty-year-old frame purposefully and fluidly. Her face looked relaxed, like she had long let go of life's bothers and worries.

She slipped into her comfortable mama-bear recliner. Mike sat on the couch, and I took a seat in a straight-backed chair across from him. "We just wanted to follow up on a couple of things from the other day."

"Well, sure. What's on your mind?"

Mike fidgeted on the edge of the couch and leaned in like a kid who just couldn't put up with any more adult pleasantries. "Look,

Mrs. Nance. You know why I'm here. I'm here to get to the truth about my brother. Okay?"

"I understand that." Her voice lilted with the measured calm of a woman who had years of experience with agitated men.

Although Mike's words sounded as if they had been rehearsed, I knew they were fueled by pure emotion. "I know you've got family, and I know you don't want to talk bad about anybody, but here's the way I see it. I think Tommy pulled the trigger. And I think either Chris or Jeff or both of them were either there or knew about it. And I think somebody drove my brother's car up to Wilmington and left it. And I think Paul helped make that happen. What do you think of that?"

Cynthia raised her eyebrows. "Uh . . . well . . . Now, I'm not just saying this because Chris is my son, but I really don't feel that Chris had any kind of dealings or responsibility with your brother being shot. Uh . . . I think his first knowledge of this is when Tommy took him over there to show him the body. And because it totally devastated Chris, I really don't believe that Chris saw your brother being killed. I really don't. Chris could not have stood that."

"But what about Tommy?"

Cynthia looked down at her folded hands resting gently on her lap and let the ticking clock answer the question.

In my role as "good cop," I nodded, smiled, and feverishly took notes as Mike pressed on, calmly and persistently. "Do you think if Tommy went to Paul and said, 'I'm in trouble,' Paul would have helped him get rid of that car — helped him get the scene cleaned up and then have been able to influence the investigation away from Tommy? That's my theory. I believe Tommy did it. And I believe he had help covering it up, and I believe he had help getting the cops off his back. That's what I believe."

Cynthia pondered that for a second. "Well, Tommy did have the benefit of his daddy being a deputy in Horry County and having a pretty good reputation with the Georgetown County police, so . . ."

"So, if they were looking at Tommy, they may have been influenced to . . ."

"To look the other way. I really don't . . . I know where you're coming from. And I know my thoughts that I've had through the years about my nephew. He was not kind to Chris. He wanted him around him, but I think that was mostly to pick on him and use him to do whatever. He was not . . . I don't know that Tommy . . . bless his heart, maybe he was looking for love and affection, because I don't think he ever got it from his mom or his dad. But he was very smart. He could figure things out."

"He was a manipulator," Mike said.

"Yes, he was a devious, manipulating person."

Mike raised his eyebrows and held out his palms "So, if he was in a jam?"

"He would find a way to get out of it."

"And who would he look to help him get out it? Paul?"

"Possibility. Possibility."

The two volleyed their comments with ease and deference, as if they stood together poking against a third unseen ominous opponent.

"And Paul would have the wherewithal to say to one of his employees, 'You, drive that car up to Wilmington, and Tommy you follow him up there and bring him back.'"

"Well, they were loyal and protective of Paul. If he said, Let's go to Timbuktu, they'd hop in the car and go with him. Beyond saying that, I don't know what that loyalty would entail."

By now, Mike was on a roll and kept plowing. "What do you think is the worst thing that Paul ever did? Do you think he just dabbled in dealing drugs or do you think it was worse than that?"

Cynthia sighed and looked Mike directly in the eyes. "That's kind of not a good question to ask."

Mike raised his hands in peace. "And I'm not trying . . ."

"I understand where you're coming from. You're trying to find everything you can, and I would want to do the same thing. And I'd probably be asking worse questions than you are."

"And at this point it doesn't make any difference. The guy that I think did it suffered a horrible death in prison, and he got what he deserved."

"He suffered a lot. And he suffered a lot before he went to prison, because he did not have a quality life. Which makes me really sad for Tommy, because he could have been so much better. Everything was always about him and what he could get you to do for him. But I just don't know — part of me wants to say that I don't believe he would actually pull the trigger on somebody."

Mike's voice grew louder and more emphatic. "And every story I've heard about him tells me that he could. And it tells me that maybe it scared the hell out of him, and from then on maybe he didn't do anything violent like that. But I think at the time of his life — at eighteen years old — he had this influence over his cousin and this Jeff character, and everything was about him. And he comes across this traveler who has money, and says, 'I'm going to take that money. And I've got a gun and I'm going to do it.' And my brother would have been stubborn enough to say, 'I ain't giving you my money.' And everything I've heard about Tommy, I can see him standing there and doing it."

"That's a possibility, and I wouldn't say that it didn't happen like that. I have a hard time seeing anybody shooting anybody, especially somebody I know. As bad as he was, and as much as I would have liked to kill him sometimes, you just don't know what their minds are thinking at times."

"Well, this has been an interesting experience for me. As you know, this is my first visit to Murrells Inlet, and we've talked to a lot of people. And I feel like we've received a lot of half-truths. And I feel like a lot of people have not been straight up with us, including the police department and including you. But I feel like, in my heart, I know who did it, and I feel pretty satisfied with that. I just wish that somebody, knowing that all of these characters are dead, and it doesn't matter, that somebody would say to me 'You know what, I think you're probably right.'"

Cynthia nodded slowly and replied like someone surprised but somehow unoffended by the sting of a slap. "Well, I'm sorry that you think I haven't told you the truth. Um, I really am."

"Oh, I think you've told me mostly the truth. But I think there're truths that you're leaving out."

"Well, I'm the kind of person who will hesitate to accuse somebody if I don't know for sure. I'm just that way. Not that I'm lying.
But unless I know that something is black and white, I'm not going
to say it's black and white. That's just who I am. If I knew the truth
more than what I've told you, then I would tell you, because I think
you deserve that. And it doesn't matter, so to speak, whether I said
Tommy killed your brother or not, but if I don't know that he did, I
cannot honestly say that I know he killed him."

"Fair enough."

"And I don't feel like saying I think he did. I thought a lot of
things I thought were right. If I knew that he pulled that trigger and
shot your brother, then I would tell you.

"Paul used to tell me that I didn't need to know stuff. Truth is, I
didn't want to know stuff. I was shocked when I did find out all the
things he was into. I could not believe that someone I loved and
married could do those kinds of things."

"And those kinds of things being . . ."

"Run dope. Buy dope. Sell dope. Make trips to Florida, bring it
back. I mean, being in the good ol' boys' pockets in Georgetown.
And because we had a successful restaurant that made money, I
never really thought that money he had was coming from something
else. You could not have made me believe that Paul dealt in drugs. I
just was naive to the point of being stupid."

"When did you find out?"

"Basically, after he died. Little rumors before—when we divorced,
but after we divorced and after he died, I found out all kinds of
stories. All kinds of stories. That he was responsible for or he helped
with the — getting rid of — people. Those are kinds of things you
don't want to know."

"So, Paul getting rid of a car would have been . . ."

"Oh, that would have been easy." She seemed relieved that Mike
skipped right over the fact that her ex-husband likely offed a few
people.

"And if Tommy came to him and said, 'Man, I did something
really stupid.' And Paul would say, 'Okay, Tommy let's take care of

it, and I want you to come back here and go get Chris and go up there and find the body, so we can call it in. Like it was a surprise.'"

"Even that . . . why would you do that to your son? I mean, I can't say it didn't happen."

"And if you found out that Paul told Tommy to get Chris so he had a witness, you would have been really angry."

"Oh, my gosh, I probably would have killed Paul. I probably would have left him right then. But I really didn't think Paul knew anything about that."

"Did you get interviewed by the police?"

"No, and that probably would have been because of Paul. Paul would have said, 'You don't need to talk to her.'"

"Do you think they talked to Paul?"

"Oh, yeah. What he told them, I would have no idea. Because it involved Tommy, and it involved Chris, yeah, they would have talked to Paul. But they wouldn't have put that in the report."

Cynthia's phone rang, which seemed to come as a relief to her. It broke the momentum, even as she let it roll over to voicemail.

"Well," she said, setting her phone on the table next to her. "I really do hope that you hear something. Maybe God will open up something that will give you closure to this. There's just so many likelihoods that it's hard to say."

Mike wasn't willing to end the conversation just yet. "I think that somebody drove that car to Wilmington, and I don't think it was Tommy, Jeff, or Chris. I think it was somebody that worked for Paul. And that's the person I'm looking for. 'Cuz as soon as I find out who drove that car up there, I'll know a lot more."

Cynthia inched forward in her chair. "Well, if Paul did it, he's got a lot to answer to God about. And, you never know, there might be something that comes together, and God may say, 'This is what you need to look at.'"

"I kind of feel like God has given me the direction to say, 'Yeah this is right.' You just need somebody who can corroborate it. And that's what I'm looking for."

"I will say this . . . Paul's dead and gone and caused me a bunch of hell and whatever else. And he gave me three great children, but it wouldn't be beyond him to have sent your brother's car out of the county."

Mike slapped his knees, stood up, and raised his hands in the air like a ref signaling a touchdown. "That's it! That's what I was lookin' for. Thank you!"

Cynthia nodded and stood to signal that she, too, was finished. I shuffled over to her, hugged her, and thanked her.

She whispered, "I hope I haven't made too much of a liar out of myself." She tilted her head toward Mike, who was making his way to the door. "He still doesn't believe me."

I looked her in the eye and whispered back. "I trust what you say. And so does he."

She smiled. "Thank you. Y'all have a wonderful trip back home. Are you driving or flying?"

"Driving to Charleston and then flying out. But we've got one more stop to make on our way."

chapter twenty-four

As we drove away from Cynthia's house, Tom was practically bouncing in the driver's seat. "So, how'd it go?"

"Mike was in prime form. He pushed and pushed and wouldn't let her off easy." I had sprawled out in the back with what I could best describe as an adrenaline hangover.

"Hey, to be fair," Mike said, "I was calm but persistent. And I got what I wanted."

"You flat-out called her a liar."

"Those weren't my exact words. I said it much nicer than that. But she did finally admit that Paul likely helped Tommy clean up the scene and get rid of Frank's car. That's all I wanted to hear. Just someone in this town to acknowledge responsibility for something."

"That is big," said Tom. "But was she willing to say who she thought pulled the trigger?"

"No, but it seems pretty obvious to me."

"You still think Tommy did it?" I asked.

Mike sighed. "I do. It makes the most sense to me. And from what we've learned about the guy, he was messed up enough to do it."

Understandable. A convenient, plausible, even probable theory. But I still had too many questions to fully agree. Carol Williams had planted some convincing seeds of another likely scenario. So, I kept my mouth shut. This was Mike's moment of clarity. Meanwhile, my mind churned in the muck of possibilities — too many loose ends to be so definitive.

Yes, Tommy McDowell was nefarious and manipulative. We could all agree on that. His litany of misdeeds led to regular encounters with local law enforcement and a prison sentence. But did he have the guts, the gumption, or the audacity to commit murder?

It seems he harbored an insatiable lust for the rush of pulling one over on someone. He schemed. He lied. He cheated. But his documented crimes — theft, arson, fraud — did not involve physically harming another person. It could be that his official record was merely a narrow snapshot of a larger criminal portfolio. Or maybe it provided a glimpse into the mind of a distressed kid who liked to stir up trouble, but who had a faint moral boundary that even he wouldn't cross.

Tommy enjoyed the thrill of firing a gun. He liked the noise and the attention it attracted. But did that make him more inclined to turn a weapon against another human?

Were the rumors true about him taking sexual liberties with other kids? If so, were they a sign that he was an abuser and a sexual predator? Or was it something less despicable? Was he merely exploring his sexuality in a way that made his small-town peers uncomfortable, thus prompting them to start the rumors? And did those rumors have any bearing on this case?

Perhaps Tommy's most telling delinquency was impersonating an officer. As is typical with bullies, he was relentlessly and consistently impersonating something — broadcasting a reckless, bad-boy persona. Could that all have been a facade that shielded the scared, angry boy who was grappling with his sexuality? And like many bullies, whose bark and bluster upstage everything, did he manipulate others to do all the biting?

There's a good argument that Chris Nance was Tommy's primary protégé. As cousins who grew up together in similarly abusive situations, the two were like brothers. Being older, Tommy had an upper hand in influencing and manipulating Chris from the moment he was born. A high school classmate who grew up in Murrells Inlet said Chris was the meaner of the two boys — a bully in his own right with a violent temper. As an adult, Chris once got so angry — and drunk — that he drove his truck through the wall of a crowded restaurant, injuring a dozen people and causing extensive damage. Could the smoldering anger of a young teenage Chris have been stoked into a raging murderous outburst? Was he just fed up with being pushed around by Tommy to the point where he wanted to show his cousin that he could be just as tough and mean by shooting Frank?

Chris claimed he wasn't in the woods with Tommy that night, that he didn't even know anything about "the boy in the woods" until Tommy told him. He backpedaled so quickly and emphatically away from any involvement that his own father (who had his finger on the pulse of that town) accused him of rewriting history. As soon as Tommy died, Chris would have been in a position to control the narrative. And he had the charm and wily personality to pull it off.

Then along came Jeff McKenzie, an equally lost soul with the susceptibilities of a lapdog — eager to please. Tommy, no doubt, delighted in controlling his strings. On the night they met Frank, did Jeff take advantage of an opportunity to prove to his elder mentor that he was a force to be reckoned with — to prove he could cross a line that Tommy wouldn't? Did Jeff kill Frank simply to curry favor with Tommy? Maybe Tommy egged him on. Maybe they all had been fueled by drugs or alcohol.

Tina Nance described Jeff as a quiet kid who didn't wander far from home, and if he did, he tended to blend in with the woodwork. "I can't see Jeff shooting him. I really can't. He was a good boy, but he was kind of . . . odd. He was the kind of guy who stayed home and worked on his tractors."

And maybe the whole thing was an accident — a party in the woods that took a tragic turn. It's certainly plausible that one, two, or all three boys led Frank to a camping spot in the woods. Maybe they smoked some weed, drank a few beers, and one of the guys felt the need to flash his testosterone. He shows off the gun, starts waving it around, it fires, and Frank goes down. In a holy-shit-what-have-we-done frenzy, they run to Paul and ask him to help clean up their mess.

If all three boys were present and if Paul helped and instructed one of his employees to help, then they are all guilty. The law in South Carolina states, "The hand of one is the hand of all."

Regardless of who pulled the trigger, Tommy McDowell had set the stage. He'd groomed the actors. He'd rehearsed and relished his role as director and puppet master. Perhaps everything went as he'd intended, or maybe he lost control.

In the end, the theories and questions don't change anything. However, pondering them over the years has provided me an opportunity to glimpse into my own psyche and soul.

When I first took on this story in my late twenties, I felt smugly definitive about my views. It was easy for me to stand on the outside and judge, to be curiously perplexed or even outraged that someone could take the life of another human being.

I've traveled many roads and weathered many seasons since then. I've succeeded and failed and loved and lost. I've experienced the joys and anxieties of becoming a father. I've softened in some areas and become more entrenched in others. As the spouse of a woman whose only sister was murdered, I've developed more empathy for the grief of survivors and a sensitivity and aversion to violence portrayed as entertainment. And I've tasted the elation of kindness, compassion, and forgiveness — given and received.

These experiences have polished the lens through which I view this story and its main characters. Frank, Tommy, Chris, Jeff, and Paul have lived in my brain for twenty-six years. I've studied them from multiple angles and considered them in various degrees of light. And the place where I keep landing, as I do with most humans, is compassion. Not as a pass for their destructive choices, but as empathy for the people behind those choices. I can't help but see them all as scared, distressed, suffering human beings crying out for love. Kind of like me. Kind of like you.

I'm confident I could never kill anyone — the mere thought doesn't comport with my personality and worldview — but who knows? I hope I never feel compelled to go there, but I can absolutely identify with the visceral feelings that might lead to a desperate act. I have felt anger, envy, fear, greed, hatred, and the limits of my own ignorance — over and over again. Hopelessness, despair, frustration, and the desire for acceptance are woven into the fabric of our human condition.

In the spirit of compassion for that condition, we all are Tommy McDowell — conflicted, sad, angry. We all are Chris Nance — scared, enraged, and forever trying to appease his father. We all are Jeff McKenzie — lonely and trying to fit in. We all are Paul Nance — misguided, greedy, and trying to prove his worth to the world. We are all Frank McGonigle — lost, searching, and longing for acceptance — shot down by a bullet.

chapter twenty-five

"This is it. Turn in here."

Tom guided the rental car through a narrow, open gate in the waist-high brick wall surrounding the Elmwood Cemetery in Georgetown. There was no sign out front, but the rows of gravestones were a dead giveaway. The area still felt bleak and lonely, but didn't look at all like I'd remembered, except for the Piggly Wiggly across the street.

I squinted into the bright afternoon sun. "I think it's in the far corner."

Tom drove slowly over the crumbling asphalt that was only wide enough for one car. It curved to the right, past a few trees. He pulled off the path and rolled to a stop in the grass.

Dry weeds crunched under our feet — something us midwesterners were not used to in the middle of spring. And the hot air smelled of creosote and organic dusty decay.

Frank's grave was about as far back as you could go before running into a rusted chain-link fence interlaced with dried kudzu vines. For a time after Frank was buried, the green broad-leafed kudzu bloomed little reddish-purple flowers through early autumn. But over the years it withered, revealing a litter-strewn railroad track and a cluttered side street well traveled by shoppers walking back and forth to the grocery store.

This is the section where the unknowns were laid to rest. The paupers. The indigent. The nameless. Georgetown County's version of Potter's Field.

Two grit-covered stones marked Frank's grave. The one simple, ground-level white slab laid by the benevolence of Mack Williams and the county taxpayers and the other upright gray polished stone placed by Frank's parents featuring carved roses and a cross. It reads:

In loving memory
FRANK JOSEPH McGONIGLE
Kansas City, Missouri
Nov. 10, 1955–June 1982
Our son who was lost and now is found
August 2, 1991

With his finger tracing the letters, Mike soaked in the words etched in the granite before tilting his head back. With his face bathed by sunlight, he squeezed his eyes tightly and clenched his jaw.

"You all right?" Tom whispered. We looked at each other and I could tell he had the same urge I did to put a hand on Mike's shoulder or offer some sort of consolation, but we just stood there.

"Yeah . . . yeah . . . I'm fine," he said.

I rocked side to side and scratched at the dirt with my shoe. "You know, when your mom described his grave to me for the first time, she said, 'It figures Frank would end up in a place like that. He always seemed to get the dregs in life.'"

"Yup. That about sums it up."

We stood in silence for a few minutes, staring down at the stones. I squatted to get a closer look and cleared away a few weeds. I clicked off a couple pictures with my phone.

In the stillness of that moment, I felt whisked far away, like I was watching the scene from above, and some random actors were playing our roles. I saw three of us, but I felt four — two sets of brothers standing there. Our loving bond, palpable as the coastal air, transcended space and time and death. We seemed so small, so isolated, and so heavy with the resignation of unanswered questions. We had come with visions of a bold cinematic breakthrough that would herald closure. I could feel scraps of disappointment flapping in the breeze like the shredded newspaper that had become lodged in the nearby fence. Surely there had to be more. Something. Another stone to peek under. Another witness to interview. But I also sensed effervescent tranquillity rising to the surface — an attitudinal shift that sometimes only a trip to a cemetery can evoke. While there was nothing left for us to do, I knew there was something we could be — at peace. Peace with the questions. Peace with the loose ends. Peace with what was.

Tom's tentative voice rippled the stillness. "Hey, Mike. Has this trip been at all what you expected?"

Mike looked at him for a few seconds with fatigued, sad eyes. "You know, I had no expectations. But I got down here and got caught up in the story. Frankly, I'd heard about this place for years, but these characters didn't really take life for me until I got down here. Just being here and talking to these people . . . it kinda brought it all home for me."

He exhaled and looked around. "I was such a different person when all this happened. I dealt with all of those skeletons. It's something I processed a long time ago and became comfortable with, and it sucks. But our story is no different from what a lot of families have dealt with — a child, a brother, whoever — that got murdered in a violent way that didn't make any sense. It might seem like a compelling story with Frank being gone for nine years, but really it's just another story of a hideous violent crime perpetrated by a stupid asshole with a handgun that should never have been on the goddamn street to begin with."

Mike slowly shook his head and dropped his chin to his chest. Then he turned and looked at us with a wry smile and raised his left hand with his index finger extended. I imagined for a split second that this is what he looked like as a kid when he was about to reveal a big secret. "I've thought about this moment for a long time. And I brought the perfect thing for it."

He pulled his phone out of his pocket and started swiping. "About two months after Frank left home, Jerry and I went to see the Grateful Dead at Starlight Theater. A friend of ours scored us some prime seats — right up front. And toward the end of the show, they kicked into this rambling version of 'He's Gone.'

"When they started singing, Jerry and I . . . just looked at each other." Mike's words began to get pinched between a few, quick trembling breaths. "We were . . . both crying. We just hugged each other . . . 'cause we both realized at that moment that Frank was gone, and he was . . . never coming back."

Mike breathed in slowly and exhaled through his nose. He shook his head like he'd hit his reset button. "So, I found this app called Relisten that has every Grateful Dead show ever recorded." He tapped his screen a few more times and rapid-clicked a button on the side. "Here it is. August third, 1982. Kansas City, Missouri."

Mike set his phone on top of Frank's tombstone and stepped back.

And there in the brilliant afternoon sun, amid a chorus of crickets and the shrill, staccato rhythms of grasshoppers, I felt my brother's warm hand rest reverently on my shoulder. It startled me at first, but I relaxed into its comfort and wondered if Mike felt Frank's presence in a similar way.

The tiny speaker on Mike's phone emitted a comforting strain that began with a few errant guitar notes. The tinkling keys of a piano joined in. A long-ago audience began to clap along. And Jerry Garcia sang:

> *He's gone. He's gone.*
> *Like a steam locomotive rolling down the track.*
> *He's gone, gone, and nothin's gonna bring him back.*
> *He's gone.*

acknowledgments

The details of Frank McGonigle's disappearance and death set up permanent residence in my brain more than a quarter century ago — occupying thousands of hours of space on my cerebral hard drive, flitting in and out of my conscious and dream states, but mostly simmering on one of my subconscious backburners. Nearly everyone I know has heard some shred of this story. And for each of those compassionate and encouraging ears (even if you were only humoring me), I am grateful.

I have utmost respect and overwhelming feelings of gratitude for the McGonigle family, who so graciously allowed me into their lives to plunge deep into their feelings and their experiences. I know this wasn't easy — it got gritty and uncomfortable at times. Thank you for your vulnerability and for sharing your love for Frank. Thank you for trusting me.

Thank you to my loving and patient partner, Jeni, who encouraged me from our first dinner date until the final edit. I cherish your eager brainstorming mind. And your editorial tweaks helped make this a better story. Your never-wavering love continues to sustain me. And to our daughters, Lyda and Willa, thank you for listening to me gnash and lament over the writing process for your entire lives. I love you always and forever.

Thank you to my siblings who were my first (and continue to be loyal) audience members. I so appreciate the way you and your kids cajoled me into retelling the story at family gatherings. You never gave up on the dream of publication. And special thanks to my brother Tom who helped me wrestle the fragments of the narrative into a form that made some sense and then eagerly accepted the role of wingman on a research trip to Murrells Inlet. I love you all.

I still stand in awe of Carol Williams. Thank you for your wise, heartfelt, and faith-inspired intuitions. Time after time you surprised me. And when I wanted to doubt or discount what was unfolding, you patiently led me into acceptance. You've made me a believer. I will always cherish our friendship.

To Cynthia Nance and Paula Nance, you have both moved me by your strength and resilience. I am forever grateful for your vulnerability and your willingness to engage in some tough conversations and to dredge up uncomfortable topics with all the raw emotions that cling to them.

Thank you to the good people of Georgetown County, South Carolina, for your patience and eagerness to help. To Mack Williams, I'm so grateful for your sincerity, compassion, and dedication to service. To Jim Fitch at the Rice Museum, thank you for your hospitality and friendship and for your willingness to share curious background details. (And it was pretty cool for you to let me borrow your vintage Mustang convertible.) To Joey Howell, thank you for receiving my endless calls and texts and for your patience and forthrightness. And many thanks to Craig Hair; Mary Boyd at the Georgetown County Museum; Harold "Buster" Hatcher, Chief of the Waccamaw People; Robin Salmon at Brookgreen Gardens; Julie Warren at the Georgetown County Library; the crew at the Georgetown County Sheriff's Department; and those who requested anonymity.

To my dear agent, editor, and friend Delia Berrigan, you rock! Thank you for believing in this story and, more important, for believing in me as a writer and storyteller. Your keen editorial sensibilities and savvy negotiating skills made this manuscript market ready.

Thank you to Mark Olshaker and John Douglas for your guidance and encouragement.

Thank you to fellow writers Dawn Downey and Jessica Conoley for helping me dust off my original draft and breathe life back into it. Your insightful edits and critiques have made me a more confident writer.

Many thanks to the remarkable team at Steerforth Press — Chip Fleischer, David Goldberg, Anthony LaSasso, Helga Schmidt, and Devin Wilkie. Thank you for taking a chance on me. Your genuine enthusiasm and support helped make this process easy.

And thank you, dear reader, for your support of the literary arts by taking time to read my story.